T0032142

car crash

a memoir
of the aftermath

LECH BLAINE

GREYSTONE BOOKS
Vancouver/Berkeley/London

For Will, Hamish, and Henry

First published in Canada, the U.S., and the U.K.
by Greystone Books in 2022
Originally published in Australia as *Car Crash: A Memoir*
Copyright © 2021 by Lech Blaine
Published by arrangement with Black Inc.

22 23 24 25 26   5 4 3 2 1

All rights reserved. No part of this book may be reproduced, stored in a
retrieval system or transmitted, in any form or by any means, without the
prior written consent of the publisher or a licence from The Canadian
Copyright Licensing Agency (Access Copyright). For a copyright licence,
visit accesscopyright.ca or call toll free to 1-800-893-5777.

Greystone Books Ltd.
greystonebooks.com

Cataloguing data available from Library and Archives Canada
ISBN 978-1-77164-864-6 (pbk.)
ISBN 978-1-77164-865-3 (epub)

Edited by Julia Carlomagno
Copy editing for international edition by James Penco
Proofreading by Alison Strobel
Cover design by Jessica Sullivan
Text design by Fiona Siu

Printed and bound in Canada on FSC® certified paper at Friesens.
The FSC® label means that materials used for the product
have been responsibly sourced.

Greystone Books thanks the Canada Council for the Arts, the
British Columbia Arts Council, the Province of British Columbia
through the Book Publishing Tax Credit, and the Government of
Canada for supporting our publishing activities.

Greystone Books gratefully acknowledges the xʷməθkʷəy̓əm (Musqueam),
Sḵwx̱wú7mesh (Squamish), and səl̓ílwətaʔɬ (Tsleil-Waututh) peoples on
whose land our Vancouver head office is located.

Contents

car crash
noun

a chaotic or disastrous situation that holds a
ghoulish fascination for observers

The Bystander

"No matter how you twist it,
Life stays frozen in the headlights."

JOHN ASHBERY

Black Hole in the High Beams

THERE WERE SEVEN OF US: five in the car and two in the trunk. We were alive together for the final time. It was quarter to ten on a Saturday night, May 2009—a long weekend.

I was riding shotgun in the gold 1989 Ford Fairlane. The trip kicked off in the sticks north of Toowoomba, ninety minutes west of Brisbane. We were at the heart of Australia's Deep North. I was short and soft-bodied with a black mop, a poet moonlighting as a jock.

Tim sat back middle. He was broad-shouldered and short-haired like Will, back right. Henry was in the seat behind me, tall and thin. He had the same blond hair and blue eyes as Dom, the driver. Hamish—pale and lanky, with thick black hair—was in the trunk with Nick, brown hair above a squat frame.

It was our final year of high school. Tim and I went to St. Mary's, a Catholic factory of athletes—boys only—in the western suburbs. The others went to Downlands, an elite coed school on Toowoomba's north side.

Up front there was nothing between the road and me except the windshield and thin air. The speakers blasted "Wonderwall" by Oasis, an elegy inside a sing-along. My memory is a blinking mix of lyrics belted out incoherently and the stink of alcohol, sweat, and cigarettes—a million things and nothing in particular.

We stopped at a new set of traffic lights. To our left was the city. To our right was the town of Highfields, one of the fastest-growing subdivisions in a carved-up country. Nuclear families hid from chaos on quarter-acre sanctuaries, safe from talk-radio-fuelled rumours of refugee gangs and possible mosques.

When the lights blazed green, we turned left onto the New England Highway. The speedometer rose progressively towards high speed. Streetlamps streaked by. The road, half-lit and disappearing, burnt a blur into my brain.

My brand-new iPhone vibrated. A message from Frida. Our courtship was at a critical phase—tomorrow afternoon, we were going to the movies before a party at a mansion on the Great Dividing Range.

There was a swift change in our direction. My gaze shifted between the competing sheets of glass. We'd drifted onto the shoulder of the highway. The back tire drifted from the road, spinning out in the mouth of a gravel driveway.

This was the split second of our unravelling.

Dom reefed on the steering wheel, a knee-jerk attempt to regain control. We slid in, out, and in again. He'd overcorrected an overcorrection. A stream of images flickered in the windshield. Road half-lit by headlights. Windshield filled with branches and leaves belonging to the median strip. A dark front yard at the start of a farm.

It took us three seconds to travel from the gravel back to the maze of nature. The Fairlane ploughed to the wrong side of the highway. By rights I should've been the bullseye, but the vehicle scraped a tree stump within the median strip, spinning us another ninety degrees.

Screams howled from the back seat as we flew into a flood of high beams. *I'm dead*, I thought. Then it hit: another car, speed meeting speed, like two protons colliding.

I didn't get the luxury of a concussion. There was a glimpse of black as my head reeled from soft impact against the dashboard. After that, everything went berserk. Liquids pissed from engines. Radiators hissed with steam. Car alarms outscreamed one another. Wipers whipped across the shattered windshield.

The hood blocked vision of what we'd hit. A sticky fluid pooled around my ankles. *I've pissed myself*, I thought. My hairy toes floated in the foam from a six-pack of beers. I wiped blood that wasn't mine onto the sleeve of a new sweater and searched frantically for my iPhone, finding it down beside the seat adjuster.

Sick sounds issued from the lips of four friends in the grip of oblivion. Dom lay face-down on the steering wheel. The back seat was a mess of erect necks and flaccid limbs. I reached out and shook Tim's arm, calmly and then much more urgently.

"Oi!" I yelled. "Wake up!"

This will go down as the loneliest moment of my life.

A heavy guy appeared at the driver's side window.

"Shit!" he said. "What happened?"

"I don't know," I said.

"Can you turn the car off?"

I hadn't noticed the Fairlane's engine still revving. I reached for the keys, but the ignition was missing. It was hidden in the plastic mess where the steering wheel used to be.

"I can't," I said.

The man fished under the hood and stilled the motor. "HEY, CHAMP! Everything's gonna be fine!"

The door handle had been obliterated. The window winder was gone. Mine was the only window still intact. I was trapped in a fast-moving disaster, each new fact more startling than the last.

A team of swift Samaritans assembled, divvying the injured between them. An off-duty nurse joined the man at the window.

"Get me out of here!" I screamed.

"Sweetie," she said, "I need you to sit still. Is that something you can do for me?"

I nodded dishonestly, no intention of playing hero and staying inside a portable slaughterhouse. I scanned for an exit route and found one through the driver's window.

The woman's eyes went wide. "No! Don't!"

I pitched my hands into the void across Dom. The first responders yanked me to safety. My feet hit the bitumen with relief. I scooted to the trunk of the crushed Fairlane.

"Wait!" said the man, or the woman, or maybe someone else.

The back cavity had been ripped open like a tin of tuna. Hamish reclined against the bumper, eyes closed. A woman rubbed my shoulder.

"He'll be okay," she said.

I searched below, above, and beside the trunk.

"We're missing someone," I shouted.

"Another one?"

I located Nick thirty feet away, lying parallel to the fog line, pupils facing up towards his brain. A crooked Z was carved between hairline and eyebrow. The glow from my iPhone revealed the white shock of his skull.

"Ambulances are coming," said a stranger.

Sirens wailed faintly to the north and south. A dozen genderless bodies moved through the lunar gloom.

"Hang in there, mate!" I yelled, clapping to boost the morale of the newcomers. "You'll be right!"

Blood gushed unabated from Nick's cranium. The lips of a first responder dripped with it, due to performing CPR on an unconscious passenger. The man dry-heaved.

SOON, THE DEAD END of the highway was alive. Cones of red and blue spun on the road like strobe lights. Fire engines. Police cars. Ambulances. An endless stream of hi-vis men and women pirouetted between each other seamlessly. They relieved the first responders of responsibility and herded the bystanders away.

My main impulse was to put some distance between my body and the wreckage. Barefoot, I was careful not to stand on broken glass. I noticed a cattle dog trying to slide its paws into the bitumen and picked up its leash. The animal could be my alibi.

A mob of onlookers swarmed from parked cars and neighbouring acreages, drawn like mosquitoes to LEDs erected at opposite ends of the crash site. Nobody seemed to connect me to the catastrophe.

Beside me was a man in boxer shorts and flip-flops. He gripped his jaw like it might fall off if he let go.

The dog whined. The sirens went quiet, or I stopped hearing them. Spotlights glimmered like twin midnight suns. I heard the same ringtone sing from different phones. Ambulances left. Sirens started again. More bystanders arrived, feigning indifference.

"So what do you reckon happened?" the man asked.

The Fairlane's roof was pitched into a tent, doors bent off their hinges. Blood covered what was left of the rear windshield. Strangers in yellow jackets and white helmets liberated Dom—now conscious—from the driver's seat.

"No idea," I said.

An eavesdropper strode over. "I got right up close," she said. "Hooligans. Kids no older than fifteen, I reckon. *Drunk.* Probably on *drugs*! I just feel sorry for the other guy."

Only now did I really *see* the other vehicle. It was a blue Holden Viva. The driver was an old guy sitting on the bitumen, face cut up and bathed in blood.

News crews and freelance photographers beat most of the emergency workers to the scene. They were voyeurs for hire, capturing proof of the accident before the trauma cleaners arrived to scrape it from the highway.

The cattle dog was gone. I wandered in the general direction of the city. The vista was a Milky Way of witnesses. Blank faces framed by dark glass. Cars flanked by unlit farmland, no stars in a silver sky. My bones glowed with guilt. Police diverted drivers to the other side of the highway. Horns blew so far and wide they were like a cathedral organ. How had I not heard that shrill sound until now?

"Are you all right?" asked a police officer behind me. He nodded sympathetically towards the wreck. "You were in the car, right?"

"Yep," I said.

We walked back towards the glowing dome. I hadn't even *left*, I realised, only making it sixty feet or so from where the staring witnesses were cordoned off by police.

"Let's get you some privacy," said the officer, eyeing the photographers.

We ducked behind some gum trees. The path was red dirt and gravel. Weeds tickled my knees.

"So, what school do you go to?" he asked.

"St. Mary's," I said.

The cop explained that he used to be a rugby union coach at Downlands, so he knew five of the passengers. This was his last shift before retirement.

A female police officer was waiting beside a fire engine with a kind smile and a hand poised to take notes.

"What happened?" she asked.

The story poured out of me in breathless declarations of innocence. "I was just looking at my phone and then saw the trees and next thing you know we skidded and got hit and I don't know who hit who or which way we were going or whose fault it was IT ALL HAPPENED SO QUICK you know what I mean?"

"We know you're still in shock," she said. "You don't need to solve everything for us right now."

The police left me. I sat cross-legged on the blacktop. A shopping bag flapped from a barbed-wire fence like a jellyfish trapped in a shark net.

The police radioed the IDs of passengers, so phone calls could be made to their parents. They eventually returned with a blanket and bottled water.

"You can go home," said the woman.

I gave them my sister's mobile number. Hannah was asleep half an hour away, but she sounded less surprised to hear my voice than might be expected.

"I've been in a car crash," I said.

Nothing about my tone suggested anything more serious than a minor traffic collision, but already Hannah was crying on the other end of the line.

"It's gonna be fine," I said.

The ambulances had left and most of the bystanders were gone. The news crews kept chasing the most gripping image. The only passenger still at the scene was lying sideways in the back seat of a police car with his eyes squeezed shut. I wasn't tired, but I couldn't bear staring at my reflection in the plexiglass.

• • • •

SUDDENLY, MY HYSTERICAL SISTER was drumming her knuckles on the darkened glass. We hugged on the highway. I sat in the back seat of her boyfriend's grey Toyota Camry. I was starving and needed to piss, but there didn't seem a sensitive way to mention this.

"The police told me you should go to the hospital to get checked out," said Hannah. "They told me there's complications that can come up even if you feel fine now. Lech, they said it's not looking great for some of your friends. What the hell happened?"

My sister stared in the rear-view mirror, seeing a person where a ghost was supposed to be. We had the same big mouths and dark brows. People who didn't know the elaborate history of our secretive foster family told us that we were indistinguishable.

"The car came out of nowhere," I said. "Like a shooting star."

"This isn't literature, Lech. It's real life!"

"They'll be fine," I insisted, and this seemed to settle the matter for the time being.

We climbed over the suburb of Blue Mountain Heights and began our descent into the city. It always amazed me how big Toowoomba looked from the north. My hometown was built in the crater of an extinct volcano. Streetlamps to the north, south, and east of the city streamed into the beaming sinkhole of the city centre. The lights sprawled west before flattening and then blacking out.

"You should call Tim's parents," said Hannah.

I dialled my best friend's number off by heart. His blonde, bubbly mother answered the phone. The police hadn't been able to reach her.

"Hey, Linda," I said. "It's Lech."

"Lech," she said. "Do you guys need a lift home?"

"We were in a car crash."

She laughed uncertainly. "Is this one of your pranks?"

"No. He wasn't in a good way. But he'll be all right."

Linda probably pictured a heavy concussion and a broken collarbone. She thanked me and hung up to get dressed.

The Camry idled at a red light beside the Blue Mountain Hotel. In the shadows stood the original Blue Mountain, peak half-eaten by an open-cut quarry. Soon the only mountaintop in the area would be on the neon signage of the rundown pub.

We flew along a silent main street, passing the tree-lined driveway of Downlands on the left. Eighteen months earlier, Nick had been imported there from St. Mary's on a sports scholarship. Thanks to him, Tim and I had been consorting with the sons and daughters of old money.

I realised that Hannah's frowning boyfriend wasn't driving west, but ahead, towards the centre of town.

"Where are we going?" I asked.

"The hospital," she said. "Mum and Dad are meeting us there."

My parents were still officially married but slept in separate suburbs. I hadn't rung them, fearing his anger and her nervousness. "Why would you tell them?" I asked.

In the mirror, Hannah looked irritated. "Did you see the news crews at the crash site? Everyone in Australia is going to know tomorrow."

Toowoomba Hospital became a leviathan at night, shadows filling the gaps. Hannah and her boyfriend waved politely at my parents before motoring away.

The loveless couple stood beneath the bright red glow of EMERGENCY. Mum was frequently taken by strangers to be my dad. She had short grey hair and large glasses. Nobody misgendered my father, a three-hundred-pound bartender. He had a thick white handlebar moustache and fists the size of baseball gloves.

"Hey," I said.

Mum hugged me. "Baby!"

Dad shook my hand with a nervous firmness. "G'day, mate!"

Both burned with questions.

"It came out of nowhere," I said.

"Oh, Lech," said Mum, "those poor other parents. We're so lucky. You wouldn't have gotten in the trunk, would you?"

"I don't know. Probably."

Dad nearly spat his dentures onto the footpath. "Get off your high horse, Lenore," he said. "We've put our own kids in the trunk!"

Mum touched the blood on my sleeve softly. "Remind me to get this soaking when we get home," she whispered.

We went through the sliding doors. The waiting room was a patchwork of late-night mishap. Babies wailed. A speed freak with dreadlocks and no shirt publicised a grazed elbow to the uninterested receptionist.

"My son was in the crash," my father declared in his megaphone voice to a line brimming with injured citizens.

Every eyeball focused on me, the unblemished front-seat passenger. An elderly man with a mangled face stepped from near the front and ushered me forward. "Yaw one lucky bugger," he said. "Lucky lucky lucky."

"Step right through," said the receptionist.

The pressurised doors hissed and swung inwards. I drifted into a hallway fleshed in pale white linoleum. The next hour was a whirlwind of medical professionals pretending that there might be something wrong with me.

The radiologist leaked tears on my bloody sweater before taking X-rays of my internal organs. "When I heard," she said, "all I could think about was my son. Same age as you. You boys think you're bulletproof."

I was led back to an observation room, where Mum and Dad sat making diplomatic eye contact.

"How'd ya go?" asked Dad.

"Great," I said.

The doctor asked me a series of questions: What was my full name? The date? The current prime minister?

"Is this really necessary?" I asked. "I feel fine."

"This is all just a precaution," he said. "We need to be extra careful when there's been a casualty."

The room went silent.

Casualty.

"Someone died?" I said. "Who?"

"William," said the doctor, after a pause. "He passed away on impact."

"He's dead?" I said.

"Yes. I'm sorry. I thought you knew."

My brain felt like it had been scraped out and put back in the wrong place. There was no line of thinking that I could link with a distinct feeling.

"I need to keep going," said the doctor.

"No worries," I said.

I watched tears dribble from Mum's cheek and land on her green cardigan before expanding. "Baby," she said. "I'm just so happy that you're okay."

"I'm sorry, mate," said Dad, under pressure to pluck some words to follow hers. "That's a real bitch."

"I'm going to find Dom," I said.

I found the designated driver in a private suite. Dom had the hint of an American accent from a childhood in Wisconsin. He was shirtless, arm covered with white plaster, blue eyes bloodshot from weeping.

"What happened?" he asked.

In his confusion, Dom had given paramedics the impression that we had been intercepted by the Holden Viva, not the other way around.

"I dunno," I said. "It was so quick."

"Is everyone else okay?"

"I haven't seen them yet."

Dom's parents arrived. Dry-eyed, I left the reunited family weeping together.

Hamish was in an operating room. Henry, Tim, and Nick were in Emergency. Doctors and nurses were preparing for three comatose bodies to be air-lifted to distant cities. My friends lay stretchered beside one another, brains swelling against skulls, breathing devices exploding from throats. Their shell-shocked families were gracious, saying how glad they were I was okay.

"You silly boys," said Melissa, Henry's mother. "*Why?*"

I was a mannequin reading from a script of cheap clichés.

"I'm so sorry," I said.

Of that night, the least fatal details stick in my memory. Shiny ambulances at the end of the loading bays. The shadow of agony around swollen eyes. But I can't remember the faces of my friends, or any final sentences that I said to them before I exited.

• • • •

WHAT DOES A SURVIVOR DO after walking away from a fatal collision with barely a scratch? There are no assimilation programs for passengers like me. We get released from Emergency straight back into the tedium of the suburbs.

My parents sat in the front of the black Ford Falcon, cosplaying as a happy couple, while their son stared at the unlit suburbs slipping past. Everything familiar seemed dreamlike.

"Do you want me to slow down?" asked my father.

"I'm fine," I said.

We drove past a gaping racecourse and navigated our way through a maze of roads dedicated to trees. *Liquidambar Street. Honeysuckle Drive. Blueberry Ash Court.* This section of town was brown from drought and considered highly undesirable due to a surge of substance abuse, but the street signs evoked paradise.

"Nearly there," said Mum, with singsong frivolity.

Our six-bedroom home on Evergreen Court was the jewel in the crown of the cul-de-sac. There were no neighbours awake to gossip about my AWOL father's sudden return from marital purgatory.

Mum got my bloody sweater soaking in a tub of stain remover. "I'll make a pot of tea," she said.

My father switched on the TV. We drank discreetly from dusty china cups that hadn't touched lips since the household patriarch—the tea drinker—had departed to live in the private quarters of a rundown tavern in a rough suburb.

"It's good to be together," he said.

The family reunion was interrupted by the jingle of a news update. The 1989 Ford Fairlane flashed on screen. A banner below the anchor's chin said: TEENAGERS IN FATAL CAR CRASH.

"We understand two of the teenagers were in the trunk," the newscaster announced.

The montage was tailored for maximum shock value: a gold wreck and a blue one, blood on the shattered windshield, a close-up of a frothing six-pack, Dom getting extracted from the crushed sedan by emergency workers in yellow hi-vis and white helmets.

"The car burst into flames after rolling," the newscaster continued.

"You didn't say anything about a fire," said my father.

"Because there wasn't one."

"What a pack of absolute bullshit artists."

"Are they allowed to make stuff up like that?" asked Mum.

The update segued into reports about bankrupt Americans, Asian swine flu, and Australian sport.

"You're up to date," said the anchor.

"Stick it up ya date, dickhead," said my father, switching off the TV.

My parents watched me polish off half a loaf of banana bread that Nick had left in our fridge after a rugby union game the previous afternoon.

"I'm going to bed," I said.

"Goodnight, baby," said Mum. "I love you."

"I'm just a phone call away," said Dad.

"No worries."

There was a two-bedroom granny flat attached to the house, where my musty bedroom sat at the end of a long hallway. I collapsed onto the mattress and scrolled compulsively from the beginning of Will's Facebook wall until the end. I was grinning in his profile picture. We appeared together repeatedly—in a taxi, at a party near the waterbird habitat, drinking Slurpees from 7-Eleven.

During the December summer holidays, he had invited me to stay at his sister's unit in Mooloolaba. The road trip to the Sunshine Coast was my final long drive with my learner's licence.

"Keep both hands on the wheel, ya bloody lunatic," my father had roared, as I drifted carelessly onto the rumble strips of a six-lane highway at seventy miles an hour.

The unit was part of an old duplex. Will, Henry, Dom, Nick, and I sat on tattered couches in the garage and drank beers from a cooler until the ice thawed into lukewarm water. We had roughly eleven months to go before Schoolies Week, our week-long graduation festival and a nationwide coming-of-age ritual.

"I wish Schoolies started tomorrow," said Nick.

"Patience, mate," said Henry. "Patience!"

"Remember: it's about the journey, boys," said Will, while peeling the label from a finished bottle. "Not the destination."

"Let's go to the beach," said Dom.

"*Let's go to the beach*," said Henry, a budding actor, in a pitch-perfect impersonation of Dom's accent.

"That's not what I sound like!" Dom protested.

"*That's not what I sound like!*" mimicked Nick, in a rendition much worse than Henry's.

At the beach, there was a white moon in a navy sky, making the water look like TV static. Night waves sprayed white noise far and wide. I was afraid that my decision to stay at St. Mary's might leave me out of the summer to come.

"Sorry to be a dog," I said.

"Who gives a shit?" said Will. "You're one of us."

Will picked up the guitar and strummed Pearl Jam songs until the sky dimmed into a cartoonish blueness.

Now Will was dead. What would the audience think of me, the survivor, if I didn't express grief without delay? At 3:10 AM, I posted my first post-crash Facebook status.

RIP Will... You can pull through boys!

In the cautious morning, before sleep, I relived the vivid string of minutes that delivered me to the headlights.

iGrief

O N SUNDAY MORNING, I was woken up by my iPhone vibrating against the lavender sheets with a backlog of missed calls and text messages.

RU ok?

Thank god your ok

RIP Lech :(

One of the rumours spreading across Toowoomba was that I'd been driving the vehicle and had died on impact. Allegedly dead, I made some awkward calls. Girls in my social circle were marshalling mourners across the city. A small group, aimless in their bereavement, had formed a vigil outside the hospital.

"You should be here with us," one told me.

In the hallway, I listened to reports blaring from the TV. "It's a tragedy sure to rock this tight-knit community," a sentimental anchor declared to my couch-bound mother from a studio on the east coast. The spectacle was wrung out for the rest of the long weekend.

I fled to the hospital, driving under blue skies without inhibition about operating a motor vehicle. Outside Emergency, a group of shivering teenagers hugged one another, between checking their phones for Facebook updates.

"Lech!" shrieked a girl from Downlands.

My existence was the subject of disbelief. I hadn't been touched this vigorously since retiring from contact sport.

"You're a miracle!"

Vincent was the blond-haired, blue-eyed school captain of Downlands. He gave me a bear hug. I liked Vincent well enough, but I wasn't a fan of physical contact with other men, unless rugby league provided me with an alibi.

"Sorry," he said, apologising for my visceral resistance.

"No worries, mate," I said. "Appreciate it."

The group provided updates. Henry was at the Royal Brisbane. Tim was at the Princess Alexandra. Their conditions were categorically *critical*. Nick was in a *critical but stable* condition at Gold Coast Hospital. Dom was in a *serious but stable* condition behind one of the tinted windows above us.

I stood on the sidewalk nodding at terms I didn't understand. *Critical. Serious. Stable.* A phrase kept ringing above the din of medical lingo: *induced coma.* But one passenger was missing from the updates.

"How's Hamish?" I asked.

My question received a collective gasp.

"He passed away," said Vincent.

"When?"

"Earlier this morning."

"He's dead?"

"We thought you knew."

"Nope."

I'd only known Hamish for a few months. At the end of March, to celebrate receiving my probationary driver's licence, Tim and I had driven to Brisbane on a whim, to watch a rugby game.

"Passing your test is hands down the nicest thing you've ever done for me," said Tim, whose birthday wasn't until spring.

The Downlands First XV rugby union team were playing St. Laurence's at Suncorp Stadium, a 52,000-seat concrete coliseum. Nick was the star Downlands player. Outside the grounds, we waited among supporters bussed in from Toowoomba.

Henry spotted us. "Look what the cat dragged in. A couple of Mary's boys." He introduced me to Hamish, whose face was baked with sun from playing cricket.

"Cool your jets, fellas," said Hamish. "Let's give peace a chance."

Hamish watched events with serious eyes and a sly grin. He seemed comfortable letting those with louder voices lead the conversation. We discovered that we both came from the same obscure rural town, Wondai, two and a half hours north of Toowoomba. My parents had run the pub there; his folks were farmers.

"I'm a diehard Wondai Wolves supporter," he said.

"My old man used to be the president of the club!" I said.

"Did we just become best friends?" asked Hamish, quoting Will Ferrell in *Step Brothers*.

"Yep!"

• • • •

AT THE HOSPITAL, the morning-after vigil agreed to relocate to Downlands. It was like driving into Hogwarts. I slowed to let a rabbit hop from the bitumen onto the grass. At the end of the long, tree-lined driveway, I parked far enough away that none of the grievers could see my battered 1993 Mitsubishi Lancer.

The courtyard quickly filled with sixty or seventy students, parents, and teachers. Bouquets had been laid on the brick steps. Candles burned in the breeze. A priest did the rounds, offering the opportunity to reconnect with God.

Occasionally, a newcomer arrived and received confirmation that the condolences proliferating across social media weren't a prank, stunning them into brief seizures of grief.

The distraught were absorbed into the prevailing mood of sad astonishment. I hovered, shaking hands and nodding as wanly as a war veteran.

"I'm gonna stick strong for the boys," I said, over and over.

Fifty people asked the same question: *What happened?* I told them the first I knew of the accident was the windshield filling with trees. I tried to allay suspicions. The car was overloaded, sure, but Dom wasn't drunk or speeding.

"It could've happened to anyone," I said.

My diplomacy was interrupted. A student ran down the driveway with his middle finger lifted to an idling four-wheel drive. It was plastered with logos for one of the commercial television networks. A blonde reporter was halfway to the courtyard. "I'm so sorry for your—"

"Piss off!" the guy shouted. "Vultures!"

The rattled reporter retreated to the car, heels tapping against the bitumen. I cringed at the meltdown, but was determined to show a calm face to the deranged situation.

• • • •

VINCENT OFFERED TO HOST a private wake at his place and rode there with me later that afternoon.

WELCOME TO PRINCE HENRY HEIGHTS!

To the left was a steep quarry. To the right was a national park. The road narrowed to a tight stretch, like a drawbridge. Vincent's house was an architectural masterpiece. It was split to accommodate gradients, walls colour-coordinated with the trunks of gum trees.

The homeowners were blond and soft-voiced, BMIs kept low by organic-based diets and gym routines.

"Let us know if there is anything we can do," said Vincent's father.

"Anything at all," said his mother.

Vincent and I were left to decompress on the patio, where the cattle dog from the crash site materialised.

"Hey, Rosie," said Vincent, hugging what was actually a family pet, before descending into a weeping mess.

Vincent was the youngest of three brothers, but university-educated parents hadn't shamed the emotion out of him. I patted the cattle dog to do something with my hands that didn't involve providing comfort to Vincent.

"Keep your chin up, mate," I said.

As night fell, parents dropped a stream of newly licensed drivers to the eco mansion. We congregated in the cinema room. Vincent put on the third *The Lord of the Rings* as a tribute to Hamish. "Catapult!" fellow fantasy fanatics shouted, breaking the spell of sombreness. I'd never seen the movies, but it felt good to be doing something with my lips besides grimacing.

Our faces were lit in the competing glow of smartphones and a sixty-inch TV. Fantasy on the flatscreen, grief in our newsfeeds. I had thirty-one Facebook messages, eighteen wall posts, fifty-seven friend requests. A memorial page for Will and Hamish brimmed with inside jokes and grinning images of the victims.

At 8:45 PM, I posted my second public statement.

RIP Hamish, I wrote. *My thoughts are with your family.*

Then Vincent made an announcement: Henry was unlikely to survive the night. His brain had pressed against the cranium before bulging back towards the spinal canal. Doctors had drilled two burr holes through his skull.

I let out a sob, but the emotion behind it dissipated. Someone paused the movie. The room stared at me.

"Let it all out," said a girl I'd never met before.

"Excuse me," I said, fleeing to the front porch.

The entire vigil followed me outside and took turns patting my back while pledging compassion. I tried to produce some counterfeit tears for a tight-knit clique of sympathisers. None came.

"You're so brave," said a stranger.

I drove home alone, the last person awake in the west.

• • • •

ON MONDAY MORNING, I sat in the kitchen slurping cereal while flicking furiously through the *Toowoomba Chronicle*. A box on the front page contained basic facts about the accident beneath the headline HORROR CRASH KILLS TEENAGERS. There was a quote from the regional police chief: "In a place like Toowoomba, everyone will know someone affected by this tragedy. It will ripple through the entire community."

Toowoomba was the definition of a big country town. People justified voyeurism with an intimacy that didn't exist—I couldn't have named a neighbour on my dead-end street at gunpoint. Nobody knew anyone, really.

To capture the wreckage from the most dramatic angle, the photographer had crouched behind the trunk of the Fairlane. The vehicles were way more crumpled than I remembered. My dead friends were pictured beside the wrecks in their school uniforms, smiling naively.

My mother appeared from the laundry room. She smelled of Rexona deodorant and menthol cigarettes. "Did you read it? They're saying it was caused by alcohol, and that the driver was speeding. Now I don't know who to believe."

"Not them," I said.

I didn't think Dom had been speeding or drinking—but maybe this just proved the unreliability of my perceptions.

Inside, I saw my face grinning from the bottom of page 2. *LECH BLAINE, 17—Minor Injuries.*

The others ranked above me. A close-up of the Fairlane was on the third page, beside a photo from the school vigil. The photographer had escaped detection with expertise, snapping dazed teenagers from a distance, surreptitiously, like we were gangsters at a graveside.

A Subaru dealership seized prime advertising space. There was an eye-catching graphic of the four-wheel drive gliding along a highway, grey and gleaming, a car that you couldn't dream of dying inside. *$33,884 drive-away.* The price was printed in the same shade as the bloodstain on the headrest of the Fairlane.

• • • •

THE TIRES OF MY FATHER'S manicured 2009 Falcon hit the driveway. He reeked of Diet Coke and Joop! cologne. We set off on a tour of Queensland's best intensive care units. The events of the previous day indicated that I should have been scripting my goodbyes, but I felt unreasonably confident that my surviving friends would make it.

The static of talk radio spat from the speakers. Brian from Dalby was welcomed onto the line. "What about these hooligans on the weekend? Lock up the driver, I reckon."

"Good call," said the shock jock. "Thanks, Brian."

Dad reacted sluggishly. We made it halfway through the next call before he inserted a Beatles compilation.

"Opinions are like arseholes," he said. "Every prick has one."

Tim was in Princess Alexandra Hospital, on Brisbane's east side. The waiting room smelled like a cross between a florist and a bakery, as visitors came armed with bouquets and cakes.

"You're a miracle!" said Linda, hugging me.

She introduced me to aunties and uncles as Tim's best mate, and the front-seat passenger. My condition winded them. I would've killed for a set of crutches.

"You should buy a lotto ticket," said one.

Tim and I had always been opposites. His bedroom was obediently clean; mine was a mess. He wanted to join the army after finishing a bricklaying apprenticeship; I dreamed of being a left-wing politician.

I went into the hall with Linda. "He's also got a bruised lung and fractured vertebrae," she said, "but they're the least of our worries."

The Glasgow Coma Scale is an international system used to evaluate the severity of head injuries. Fifteen is fully awake. Three is basically brain-dead. Straight after the crash, Tim was given a GCS rating of three. This had improved to five after hospital admission, but 90 per cent of patients with his extent of neurological damage remain in a persistent vegetative state.

"They need to give his brain a breather, you know?"

"Yeah," I said. "Sure."

We were operating on different wavelengths. I was more worried about whether Linda would let Tim attend graduation parties after the concussion lifted.

Linda pressed a bell to summon assistance from the nursing station. I rinsed my hands with the disinfectant before the nurse took me through to Tim's bed.

He discharged the same schoolyard scent. I moved close enough to touch him, but didn't. A hole had been drilled through his throat for a thick hose. Blue and white tubes ran from the mouth and nose. His sealed eyelids were wet, as though he'd been crying. I stared at Tim for fifteen minutes, and gnashed my teeth to muffle an embarrassing flood of despair.

In the waiting room, I hugged Linda. Her words dripped with nostalgia for a past so recent yet irretrievable.

"You two were good boys," she said. "Weren't you? You knew how to have fun. But you were *good*."

"Tim's a good guy," I said, unsure about myself.

"I never imagined this. Not in a million years. I'm praying to God, Lech. I beg for a miracle. Will you pray for Tim?"

"Yes," I lied, a second-generation atheist. "I'll pray for him."

My father and I retreated down the Pacific Highway to the Gold Coast. There was heavy traffic on all eight lanes as people headed home at the end of the long weekend. Dad parked on the street outside the hospital, a lime hinterland climbing above the horizon.

Nick's father, Steve, was in the smokers' area. He had managed the rugby league team that Nick, Tim, and I once played for. The tough truck mechanic hugged me while sobbing.

"Nick's so messed up," he said.

I followed him into the waiting room. Nick's mum, Anne, was a short public servant with a jet-black bird's nest. Mascara was smeared around her eyes, but she remained in control, providing a precise inventory of Nick's tongue-twisting injuries.

Nick had a GCS rating of six, one better than Tim, with brain swelling and two small hemorrhages. Bruised lungs and broken ribs. On impact, the tendons on his right hand had been slashed cleanly. His ring finger had snapped in half, piercing the skin.

"Trust you to get in the front seat," said Anne, "and Nick to get in the trunk. He's always been the loose cannon, hasn't he?"

Nick and I had met at St. Mary's as ten-year-olds. I'd just transferred from a tiny public school to a frightening new world of navy ties and Hail Marys. I spent the first morning break sitting alone and trying not to cry or shit myself.

"What's your name?" asked Nick, clinically disinhibited.

"Lech," I said, preparing for the explanations. "It's Polish."

"Cool," he said, mercifully.

For the next ten minutes, my first friend at St. Mary's tried with increasing success to make me piss myself with laughter.

Anne led me through dark hallways. The grim facilities made me less confident about the patient's prognosis, even though he was much closer to life than Tim.

By flying from the trunk while crossing the median strip, Nick had avoided a final, fatal ricochet of grey matter. A drip spiked from the peak of his freshly shaved skull. He looked like a comatose Harry Potter.

"You saved him," said Anne. "The doctors reckon that he could've bled to death if you weren't there."

"No," I said.

"I'm serious!" she said. "He owes you his life. *We* owe you."

I waited for ages with my hand on the metal railing, so tired that I felt no guilt about my inability to cry.

That night, the highway was a ghost route. AM radio played the best of the eighties. Billboards advertised the right to life, lies writ large in the headlights. *ABORTION IS A SIN! JESUS IS COMING!*

The patriarch's mobile phone lit up with extended family who'd heard The Bad News. He received a call from my cousin, Allan Langer, a rugby league player famous for punching above his featherweight frame. Dad's eyes flicked to his limp-wristed son. "He's a tough little bugger," he said. "Don't you worry about that."

I watched the side-view mirror with a sinking feeling. Semi-trailers dribbled away in small, colourful blinks.

Dad cleared his throat of phlegm, lowered the window, and spat out the side of his mouth strategically.

"I was really proud of you today, mate. To show your face like that. I don't know what I would've done if..."

His bloodless knuckles gripped the steering wheel.

"Just remember that I'm gonna be here for you. Right?"

I kept my eyes straight and breath steady. The range was black tape reeling between ground and clouds.

"No worries," I said.

Dad turned up the radio. I unlocked my iPhone with the urgency of an asthmatic. It hadn't stopped vibrating between hospital visits. Hundreds of acquaintances and strangers sought a subscription to the ongoing soap opera of my survival.

I went through and accepted every friend request, mistaking curiosity for kinship.

Others spammed my wall with digital chitchat.

heyy im so sorry about the crash :(i hope u dnt mind the random add im michelle btw im 16 and live in toowoomba. my msn addy is sxc_babe789@hotmail add me :)

sorry about your friends :(they seem like great guys

hey i hope your ok nobody deserves what your going thru!!!

The memorial page had ballooned to more than one thousand members, with hundreds of wall posts. There was little to distinguish the rubberneckers from the genuinely bereft. Strangers pleaded for medical updates and gave heartbreaking accounts of exaggerated relationships. Trolls preached about evil teenage drivers, provoking moral condemnation from others.

Family members of the dead explained with harrowing detail the ways their lives would never be the same.

At 9:09 PM, I posted my third public statement.

Thank you to all the well wishers, I wrote. *My thoughts remain with Will, Hamish, Henry, Nick and Tim's families. If there is anyone I can help at this terrible time, please don't hesitate to get in contact with me.*

My iPhone was a bright light to be blinked at, until the blank minutes became days and nights of missing time.

• • • •

GRINNING SCHOOL ID PHOTOS of Henry, Tim, and Nick greeted newspaper subscribers on Tuesday morning. *TRIO FIGHTS FOR SURVIVAL* read the headline. For the rest of my life, I would pay spiritual attention to every newspaper article about motor vehicle mortality. These are the secret scriptures of a survivor.

After breakfast, I drove to St. Mary's. A special assembly was scheduled to update seniors and dampen spreading speculation.

The sparsely attended barbeque before the accident became a bit like Woodstock—*I was there*—transformed into an under-age rager attended by hundreds. Some claimed that they were offered entry to the trunk, but didn't cave in to peer pressure.

"It could've been my son!" said their mothers.

By the end of the day, the consensus was that we were drunk and/or high, drag-racing back to town after gatecrashing a party with baseball bats.

On the phone, the deputy principal had begged me to keep a distance, perhaps fearing that I would contaminate the campus with grief, or simply freak my classmates out. "You need a breather," he said.

I insisted on coming in. Breathers were for the weak.

The campus was far more basic than Downlands. Dense assemblies of concrete blocks and corrugated iron were set in a treeless scenery of hot blacktop.

In the hall, one hundred teenage boys gaped at my arrival. I received a round of applause. My geography teacher hugged me. This was even more awkwardly received than the one from Vincent, because it had so many witnesses. The scene was different from the day at Downlands. Will and Hamish were strangers to these students. The bleakness of Tim's condition was a secret.

I took a spare seat in the back row. The priest, kitted out in a white robe with purple trimmings, spoke about the healing effects of liturgy. "Two things in life will last," he said. "Faith and hope."

It was announced that a psychologist would be available to students for the rest of the week. To my knowledge, nobody visited. I didn't even consider it. At Downlands, the presence of girls permitted a grander level of emotional expression. St. Mary's boys were moulded into athletes and tradesmen who negotiated hardship with stiff upper lips.

The deputy principal asked half-heartedly if anyone had further remarks to make. I hijacked the microphone and delivered a bizarrely macho speech.

"It ain't over yet, boys!" I said.

The room was still reeling from news of the car crash and the secondary information that I hadn't been killed. Now I was front and centre in the main hall, rallying them. The phrase *out-of-body experience* didn't do justice to how far I'd flown from my feelings.

"Let's stick together," I said. "For Tim!"

Five hundred yards away, at a private girls' school, a delirious senior took the microphone. She claimed to be a cousin of one passenger and a girlfriend of another. She'd been at the "party" before the crash. She heard the collision happen a few hundred yards away and rushed to cradle the victim's bloody bodies.

It was emotional karaoke. Nobody in the crash had ever met her. The most unsettling thing wasn't the quality of the performances, or how deeply people believed in their forgeries of trauma. It was that complete strangers seemed more capable of feeling real grief than me.

• • • •

SINCE THE CAR CRASH, a dozen different media outlets had contacted me to address the conjecture. Some of the programs had celebrity hosts and seven-figure audiences. The producers would cold-call the house or my father's business. I came to recognise the glib sympathy: *Hope you're doing okay!* They tried to seduce me with the erotic pleasure of widespread attention.

"Social media is causing a lot of untrue rumours to spread," said one. "This is your chance to straighten the record."

I told my father that I wanted to address the rumours head-on. Less than a week after the crash, I met a journalist and a photographer from the local newspaper. I came armed with a 1,500-word essay about voyeurism that I expected to be printed, carte blanche, in the editorial section.

"I don't want any pictures," I said.

The journalist had to disenchant me gently. "Here's what you've gotta understand. My editor isn't going to print a rant. And if you don't let me take your photo, they'll just get a picture of you from Facebook."

I waved the stapled reams of paper. "I really need to address the stuff about drunk driving and speed. It's bullshit."

"This is excellently written," he said, glancing through. "I could definitely get some of this into an article."

"I don't want to do a front-page sob story."

"Well, tell me about them. Let's get the gossipers to see that they're dealing with real people here."

The journalist pressed the red button on the tape recorder. I spoke about my dead friends. The photographer clicked in the background.

"You're a bloody inspiration," said the journalist. "People are going to see a different side of this thing."

• • • •

THE FOLLOWING MORNING, a beaming celebrity tamed a snake atop the front page. *FREE: 24 wildlife cards to collect!* Underneath, the headline said EXCLUSIVE in blood-red font. *Our reporter speaks with Highfields crash survivor LECH BLAINE.*

My glum face evaded eye contact with the photographer. I looked full of shady secrets, with bags under my eyes, gazing at the miniature vignettes of Hamish, Will, and Henry. They were moons trapped in the dark orbit of my self-absorption.

WE'LL STAY STRONG FOR FAMILIES

Lech Blaine is a very lucky young man—he just hasn't taken the time to think about how lucky. Lech walked away from Saturday night's horror crash near Highfields virtually unscathed.

Rather than dwell on the circumstances of the tragic event, he has instead focused energy on his dead mates. TURN TO PAGE 3.

The portrait of my stoic survival was encircled by advertisements.

NEW SLIMMING DRINK. *Add twice a day to your favourite beverage. What have you got to lose?*

LEISURE POOLS TOOWOOMBA: *Huge Savings on Our Specials! Call 1300 SPLASH.*

WANT LONGER LASTING SEX? *Find out about nasal delivery technology. Call now for a free consultation.*

It's important that we stay strong, the reporter quoted me in the article. *The best thing at the moment is that the boys are still fighting.*

Tragedy attracts eyeballs. If it bleeds, it leads. The journalist and advertiser both win. Meanwhile, survivors feel an equal need to be seen and to disappear, to spill our guts and then cut our tongues out.

Terrible
Perfection

I SAID GOODBYE TO HENRY on Wednesday afternoon. He was dying on the fourth floor of the Royal Brisbane and Women's Hospital. The mood was much lighter than I expected, and this made me briefly optimistic. All it meant was that death had been accepted.

I hugged his mother, Melissa, in the ICU waiting room. She articulated her anguish with bitter precision. No last-minute bargains were getting thrashed out with God.

"Henry is going to die soon, Lech," she said. "We have decided to switch off his life support later today."

As the Fairlane flew across the median strip, grey matter smashed against the front of Henry's skull before rebounding, wiping out the links among his brain cells. At the crash site, he recorded the maximum GCS score of three.

I'd only known Henry for a year, but we'd become close. He was ranked fourth on my list of Myspace friends; I was ranked fifth on his. We were similar enough to kindle a swift intimacy and different enough to avoid competitive friction. Most of the guys in our clique wanted to be tradesmen, soldiers, or professional athletes. Henry and I talked about moving to Brisbane for university.

"The doctors have been extremely honest with me," said Melissa, away from the other visitors. "If Henry were to survive, it wouldn't be my son waking up. I can't imagine him wanting to live like that. Can you?"

"No," I said.

"*No.* Neither can I. It will destroy me. Nobody understands. Our connection is different, deeper."

I found her candour refreshing. Melissa didn't tell me that I was still breathing for any particular reason.

"Apart from the brain, the rest of his organs are in immaculate condition. So we've decided to donate them. I think Henry would appreciate that. Don't you?"

"Yeah," I said. "He really would."

At Downlands, Nick and Henry had quickly formed a tight bond. I became their third wheel, a beta between two alphas. We spent entire weekends together at Nick's place. I waited all week through the repetitive lessons at St. Mary's to reunite with a more dynamic life.

Melissa escorted me into the ICU. We walked through the security doors and down the bright hallways. Henry had a private room where blinds kept the sunlight at bay.

Translucent tubes, held in place with tape, ran from Henry's mouth and nose to the machines keeping him alive. There was a dense assembly of pipes, hoses, cables, and drips. His hair had been shaved during surgery to allow for the drains pumping blood away from the brain.

"Not even a scratch," said Melissa.

Henry's weight had fallen to 130 pounds—a dramatic drop. But the rest of his physical statistics were considered *unremarkable* except for the record of a grazed hand and a chipped tooth. No illicit substances were located in his system.

"I'll let you have some privacy," said Melissa.

I held Henry's hand. The screens and machinery obliterated my big words. We were both missing from the moment: him physically, me emotionally.

I whispered, "I'm sorry, mate."

In the waiting room, Melissa hugged me. "Make me one promise."

"Anything," I said.

"Never forget Henry, Lech. Never forget him."

"Of course. I wouldn't. I couldn't!"

The car trip home was the same as all the others. I listened to the tires sigh across the bitumen.

In Glenvale, dusk bathed the cul-de-sac. A game show hummed behind the lounge-room blinds. Dad didn't come in—his estrangement from Mum had recommenced. I went straight to my room and fell asleep.

I woke to a vibrating iPhone. Outside, there was a symphony of insects and jiggling cat bells spliced by the occasional *swiiiiiiiish* of a car passing not far beyond the back fence.

At 5:35 PM, an ultrasound failed to detect any blood flow to Henry's brain. His organs were removed and used to save the lives of five strangers. The only organ that counted was the brain: 3.13 pounds of nothing.

At 9:43 PM, I posted my final Facebook status on the crash. RIP *Henry!!!* I wrote. *I'm going to miss you so much mate.*

Rest in peace. It was grief expressed with the depth of a radio jingle. I was heading off allegations of indifference. It had nothing to do with Henry, or Hamish, or Will, and everything to do with me.

Maybe the grief I sought was no longer possible to *feel*. Maybe social media had made loss obsolete.

Still, I dreaded the pending tributes that would expose my friendship with Henry as fairweather. So I changed my profile picture to an image of us together. The main emotion I felt was regret that we hadn't taken more photos.

How else could I prove what I had lost?

• • • •

WILL'S AND HAMISH'S FUNERALS were on a blue-skied Friday, six days after the collision. Hamish's service was in the morning at Downlands, where he'd been a boarder since Grade Eight. I went to all three funerals with Dom, whose arm was still in a sling.

We idled along the school's driveway. In the back seat, Dom's blue eyes—still bloodshot—were focused on the scene outside. He didn't stop fidgeting. "How many people do you think are coming?" he asked.

"I dunno," I said. "Maybe a thousand."

The attendees packed the main hall and spilled out into the courtyards. Students wore blue blazers and striped ties with pins for extracurricular activities.

I'd only met Hamish half a dozen times. It felt more like decades that we'd known each other. Two months before his death, Hamish had posted the words *Wondai pride* on my Facebook wall, the only direct digital conversation that I could track down.

There were nine eulogists, including two younger sisters who also went to Downlands. Hamish's dad looked like an older, thicker version of his lanky son, sent from the future to rectify the absurdity of the situation.

I was struck by a fever of survivor's guilt and imposter syndrome. What right did *I*, the survivor, have to cry? There were hundreds of people whose sorrow was more warranted than mine. So I muzzled any public displays of pain, *toughing it out*, as my father would say, *up the guts*, like mourning was a game of football.

Vincent gave a eulogy. Hamish had savoured physical activity: cricket, rugby union, shooting, and waterskiing. But he also had an encyclopedic knowledge of Harry Potter and The Lord of the Rings. The average rugby player wouldn't confess to an obsession with fantasy, but Hamish didn't see the smart and simple sides of himself in opposition. He united the factions of tough boarders and bright day kids. The crowd laughed at a life that quietly animated the dry school environment.

Hugs failed to allay the insanity of witnessing a dead friend get carried away in a timber casket for cremation. It was all too civil. We stood together and adrift, waiting for something to give, subsumed into a communal mood of isolated astonishment.

Most of the mourners travelled in a motorcade to Will's funeral on the other side of town. Autumn leaves spun across the main street like hundreds of miniature tumbleweeds. Dom and I sat in the back seat of his parents' car. The chauffeur drove with a noticeable slowness to protect Dom's broken bones.

"I don't know what to say to people," he said.

"Just tell them that you're sorry for their loss," I said.

"But that doesn't mean anything."

"It's better than nothing."

St. Patrick's Cathedral was situated within a precinct of petrol stations and car dealerships. Fumes mixed in the musty air with incense and candle wax. The graffiti of sinful Christian kids was carved into wooden pews packed to capacity. Stragglers listened to amplified hymns from plastic seats on the front lawn, their suffering interrupted by the gear changes of trucks and buses.

Dom and I selected a pew towards the front of the cathedral. The windows were stained yellow and blue. Sunlight became blinding if you looked through the glass.

The funeral was more sombre than Hamish's. The average age of the audience and eulogists was older. We got the blunt message that Will wasn't coming back.

A logbook, an airport card, and earmuffs were placed on the coffin. A flyover of the gravesite would be performed later. His sister recited a passage that Will had written about flying. I was stunned by the depth of someone who'd seemed so down-to-earth.

Some people might say that freedom is being alone in the bush with the only sounds being murmurs from the birds, he had written, *but I believe freedom is at five thousand feet with no other sound but the engine roaring.*

In his father's oversized blazer, Dom wept with a directness that I later came to envy. "It's okay, mate," I murmured.

Outside, the sky had faded into a greyer shade of blue. News crews recorded the procession of the casket to the hearse. Young men exhaled through quivering noses, mouths closed, afraid of the sounds that might emerge if they opened them. I squirmed in the expiring sunlight.

"I'm so sorry for your loss," I said again and again, the survivor who couldn't cry.

I bluffed a thousand apologies that day, though privately I was unsure what I was sorry for. I was sorry for being so sorry. I was sorry for not being more sorry.

There was no vocabulary for the strangeness of bereavement, especially when the departed were young, the end so abrupt. We couldn't use soothing euphemisms about a good innings or going to a better place.

Hamish and Will would never get to make the mistakes that shape a character, the way people break hearts and drift apart from family members. Most of us would never trade the rifts and disappointments of adulthood for that terrible perfection.

• • • •

THE THIRD FUNERAL was on the front lawns of Downlands. It was seven days since the first two services, nine days since Henry was pronounced dead, thirteen days since the crash. I picked up Dom from his house in Mount Lofty, a quick trip from the site of the accident. We found a parking space at the school where I used to spare Henry from catching the bus back to Highfields. The morning brimmed with peculiar intensities of déjà vu and newness. Blue skies. Bouquets on a brown coffin. One thousand mourners gathered to be touched by the rituals of public suffering. We had done this all before. We had never done anything like it.

I sat with Dom and Vincent near the front. Someone clutched my shoulder. I hadn't known my father was coming. We shook hands firmly. He had taught me to make eye contact and err on the side of hurting a man's palm and fingers when shaking them.

"Keep your chin up, mate," he whispered.

My father didn't need to deliver the message. I was afraid of publicly or privately displaying favouritism, of appearing to be affected by one death more than another. So I distanced myself from physical particularities.

It's not like I've known him forever. Will and Hamish died too. It could've been worse—Nick and Tim are still alive. I could've been killed.

I diminished Henry in self-defence. Teenage boys are petrified of confessing how much we mean to each other.

Henry's photo beamed from the cover of the memorial booklet, the same image that they would use in the newspaper the next day. An oval face with a snub nose and chiselled jawline. Dimples flanking big teeth, and the trademark split dividing his bottom lip. Tan skin and a long, curling fringe that was blond at the tips—souvenirs from those summer road trips to the coast.

The priest began the Eucharist. I studied the program as though I were cramming for an exam, so that my gaze couldn't stray and make contact with anyone. The coffin was sprinkled with holy water. On top were placed a guitar, car keys, a First XV jersey and boots, and a pillowcase. We listened to psalms, hymns, prayers, and blessings. Jeff Buckley's "Hallelujah" hissed from the speakers.

"Lord, we pray for all the families affected by this tragedy," said one reader. "May your healing presence strengthen and support them in this time of need."

On the Sunday morning before Henry's funeral, Melissa had called to ask if I would deliver a eulogy. I was on the way to see Nick at the Gold Coast Hospital, after visiting Tim in Brisbane the day before. I should've politely declined. Henry had closer mates who weren't gripped by the challenge of being a stoic survivor.

My eulogy featured punchline after punchline. "Where do you start with Henry?" I said. "He was the singer of songs, the stealer of shirts, the guy with a thousand clichés, who always got the best-looking girl and never paid for a feed in his life."

I worried that my stories weren't funny enough, that there wasn't the perfect anecdote to distil the macho Casanova I believed people wanted to remember.

"Henry had many achievements in his eventful life," I said, "but there was one that outstripped all others: mounting the giant horse above the saddlery on Taylor Street late one Friday night after a few too many beers. You should've seen the size of the bloody thing!"

I presented Henry the way most teenage boys want to see themselves: funny, popular, brave, uncomplicated. It got a tremendous reception. Henry's friends were in stitches. I missed the cringing ripple among the witnesses who knew his deeper side.

Melissa was dismayed by the abbreviations. "Henry was so much more than that, wasn't he?" she asked, not bitterly, but sifting for a trace of reality.

What if I had told the audience that Henry's talent wasn't sleeping around, but having platonic friendships with women? That he didn't resist the friend zone like it was the Bermuda Triangle? That he was a son who wasn't afraid to say "I love you" to his mother, alone or in front of others?

Henry wasn't an academic mastermind or a champion athlete, but he was a genius at generating intimacy within a diverse social network, and making the people he met feel better about themselves.

I should've spoken about the marvel of meeting someone who enlarged rather than restricted my sense of self. But I downplayed the accumulation of company that can't be spun into funny stories, and the comfortable silences that define a friendship just as much as the parties.

The sun crept into the west and shone behind us. Mourners fanned themselves with memorial booklets, necks red and armpits wet. The keepsakes were removed from the coffin and more holy water sprinkled. The choir sang in Latin as the pallbearers made their delivery. A guy wearing a kilt played the bagpipes and led an idling hearse past a dehydrated guard of honour.

As Henry's body was driven to the crematorium, we retreated to the dining room for *refreshments*. Waiters lingered with plates of finger food. Grievers breathlessly estimated attendance figures.

"Henry was a popular boy," said one mother. "There must've been a thousand people here today. *At least.*"

Onlookers mistook my dissociation for maturity.

"You're a tough bugger," said the father of a friend. "That was a great speech you gave today."

"He was a great mate," I said. "I'm gonna miss him."

Spoons and teacups clattered against china. Ringtones sang from pockets amid the polite chatter and muted amusement.

The school bell blew regular reminders that life continued beyond the wake.

"You know," said one woman, "He does everything for a reason."

I munched on a sandwich. "Who's that, sorry?"

"*God.* He must have big plans for you."

Strangers expected me to do something immense, to leave a mark on the world big enough for three people.

"You are a lucky boy. Don't waste this, will you? No, I'm sure you'll do incredible things. But above all, be *happy.*"

We expect survivors to grin and bear the events that tear them apart. I encouraged these far-fetched ambitions. "I'm not going to let this gift go to waste," I said. "Henry wouldn't want me to be miserable for the rest of my life."

A few people bravely interrupted the bullshit.

"How are you *really* holding up?" a man asked. "A lot of people are going to blow sunshine up your ass. But grief isn't a kissing contest."

"It's a terrible tragedy," I said, "but I'm just hanging in there."

Hanging in there. Hanging in there. Hanging in there.

Behind my saccharine clichés was utter nothingness. I was neither holding up nor falling down, just aimlessly continuing.

Later, alone, I wondered: *Where am I hanging? What am I holding on to?*

There were no days since the accident, not in the traditional way of twenty-four-hour phases following one after the other. I had kissed goodbye to the rhyme of being alive when the possibility of happiness wasn't sabotaged by a rational sadness.

A Portrait of the Artist as a Young Larrikin

AN ARTIST DOESN'T happen by accident, and neither does a larrikin. My parents met at a backyard barbeque in Ipswich, near Brisbane, circa 1979.

Mum was a nervous bookworm and a financial clerk for a department store—a bush poetry enthusiast with a permed mullet who shunned makeup, dresses, and jewellery. She was allergic to public speaking and physical exercise.

She said, "Slow and steady finishes the race."

She said, "You're not playing for keeps."

She said, "You don't need to *win* anything to have fun."

Dad was a three-hundred-pound cab driver with a mullet and a handlebar moustache who had never read a novel in his life. A rugby league coach and a former professional gambler, he let off steam at weekends by punting large sums on thoroughbreds and greyhounds. He peppered his enemies with insults and sculled beer from a saucepan. Beating people was the meaning of life.

He said, "If you're not first, you're finished."

He said, "You need to risk it to get the biscuit."

He said, "Never trust a bloke who doesn't drink."

My father was a quintessential larrikin—Australia's national archetype of brash and brave masculinity. I have her to thank for the vocabulary and him for the ego.

Both dropped out of high school before Grade Nine to support their families. Dad dreamed of being a rich businessman. Mum dreamed of raising a big family.

After tying the knot, Mum suffered six miscarriages. The pragmatic underdogs became foster carers instead and relocated to the bush in pursuit of a cut-price Australian dream. By autumn 1991, they'd leased three rundown pubs across country Queensland and accepted six permanent foster children under the age of twelve. This brood sometimes blew out to ten or eleven.

"One more try," said Mum, who had started taking a shady estrogen-replacement drug from a rogue fertility doctor at the age of thirty-eight. It was manufactured from the urine of pregnant mares.

Secretly, she daydreamed about a baby girl named Amy Blaine, another shy female, and a rare example of her personal preference prevailing over that of her cocksure husband.

"Let's hope the piss came from Phar Lap's granddaughter," said Dad, craving a biological son who could run the hundred metres faster than a racehorse.

On January 22, 1992, I arrived to great fanfare, surprisingly alive, a miracle child with a full-blown god complex. My mother emerged from a C-section to see her first breathing baby wrapped in a pink sheet. The hospital had run out of the blue ones it used for boys.

"It's a girl!" she cried.

"Nope," said Dad. "It's a *boy*."

According to my eldest brother, Trent, it went back and forth like this: *It's a girl! It's a boy! It's a girl! It's a boy!*

Mum gestured desperately. "Why would they give a pink sheet to a boy?"

Dad unwrapped the sheet to expose the only evidence that mattered, his prize for a lifetime's supply of bad luck. "My kid's got a dick!" he roared.

My father won naming rights and named me after his doppelgänger, Lech Wałęsa, a fat battler with a thick moustache. Lech was a revolutionary trade unionist and the freshly elected president of Poland. My pop John had been a blacksmith on the Ipswich railway and vice-president of the Queensland Ironworkers Union—this was why a bartender in Wondai dedicated his long-awaited heir to Eastern Europe's great emancipator.

• • • •

AT THE AGE OF SIXTEEN, my father had shattered his hip at the Ipswich meatworks and spent six months in the hospital. He never played rugby league again. That bitter winter, Dad's brother George won the Bulimba Cup for Ipswich as a goalkicking fullback, and his sister Rita gave birth to a blond bombshell named Allan Langer.

After Allan dropped out of high school, my mother got him his first job, as a furniture removalist, while my father was still getting laughed out of clubhouses across Ipswich for suggesting his five-foot-four-inch nephew would play football for Queensland and, one day, Australia. "Are your eyes painted on?" they said. "He's a friggin' midget!"

Dad had a history-making chip on his shoulder. He was pissed off about missed opportunities, and craved greatness in the next generation of the Blaine bloodline. Allan was a part-time athlete and full-time council worker when selectors picked him to play the first game of the 1987 State of Origin,

Australia's most watched sports series. "Alfie" starred from the get-go, picking up Man of the Match in the series decider.

The year 1992 was indisputably the happiest of my father's life. On the fourth Sunday of spring, Allan captained the Brisbane Broncos to the first of consecutive premierships against the St. George Dragons, whipping the cream of Sydney's establishment.

"You little beaut-*ay*!" Dad sang while feeding me mashed bananas and himself a Johnnie Walker and Diet Coke. That scruffy Australian underdog was the father of a son and the uncle of a gun.

My parents sold the lease of the Wondai Hotel. Mum got paid a few dollars an hour to be a 24/7 psychologist to six children. Dad got a part-time job as a bartender at the Wondai Bowls and Golf Club. They ploughed their life savings into a cheap acre of red dirt, where they planted a mobile home that used to be a maternity hospital.

Every Sunday for a month, my brothers filled the bed of a one-tonne pickup with turf from the local slaughterhouse. My father drove the cargo home so they could mask the drought-stricken earth around the house. He had thick forearms and tanned, muscly calves. "Mowing the lawn's better than watchin' porn," he'd say.

At night, Mum and Dad checked my cot as though it harboured a million-dollar bill. During the day, six overprotective foster siblings studied every burp, piss, fart, and shit with wonder and unspoken envy. "Mum," they cried, fighting over me. "It's my turn to hold him!"

The slew of days and nights turned me into a toddler, but my novelty didn't wear off. I remember an island of green grass in an ocean of red dirt. The sound of buzzing flies and squealing springs on a trampoline. The scent of beer on Dad's thick, tickling fingers, and the whiff of menthol cigarettes from Mum's insistent kisses.

"Mummy didn't have any babies come from her tummy until a little boy named Lech Jack Thomas," she cooed, a lullaby that never grew old. "Everyone was so happy the day that Bubby Jack was born, but especially Mummy and Daddy. He made up for the sad times, because his face made Mummy feel warm and fuzzy in the tummy."

The adoration was unsustainable. I'd never be loved so unconditionally again. This set me up for daily heartbreaks in the real world, where no one responded with quite the same level of amazement.

We moved to Toowoomba in 1996. My father bought a cheap hotel lease. My mother—who didn't want to leave the bush—ferried six foster children in a small bus. Dad and I drove separately. I sat in the front passenger seat of a black Ford Falcon with a moon roof. We passed farms that hadn't yet been subdivided, and the slight bend in the highway where my life would spiral out of control.

Toowoomba was treated to its wettest year since 1893. I remember pissing rain and hissing winds. The Country Club Hotel was stubbornly rundown, a fitting reflection of the suburb, Mort Estate, which was filled with boarding houses and council flats. The customers were tradesmen and railway workers with loose bowels and foul mouths. They drank cheap schooners of beer until the sun went down. Then the shot glasses came out and their red necks got hot underneath blue collars.

"Oi, two-pot screamer," my father declared to a drunk man speaking lewdly to the barmaid during happy hour. "Pull your head in, before I do it for ya."

I was forever running from the bartender to the bookkeeper. In the office, my mother kept a secret stash of sweets. She raised seven kids while speed-reading half a dozen novels a week, and could recite "The Man From Snowy River" and "Clancy of the Overflow" verbatim, like a bush poetry jukebox: "*the hurrying people daunt me, and their pallid faces haunt me. As they shoulder one another in their rush and nervous haste.*"

We had matching hazel green eyes and generalised anxiety, but my mother was never the same after moving to the big city. She didn't like the density of bodies and the condescension of rich agricultural types from old money. During the wettest year since Federation, mosquitoes provided a convenient alibi for clinical depression—she blamed lethargy on Ross River fever.

Although Dad had the gift of the gab, he was minimalist, not a chatterbox like me.

He said, "Life's a mixed bag of shit."

He said, "Death's a one-horse race."

He said, "Pity's the last straw of pride."

My father's poisons of choice included steak-and-bacon sandwiches, sausages, rissoles, T-bones, lamb cutlets, rib fillets, deep-fried potatoes, meat pies, and sausage rolls. I never saw him eat so much as a chicken nugget or a fish finger, such was his fidelity to red meat.

"Chicken's for women," he told me. "Fish is for Christians."

"What about salad?" I asked.

"Do I look like a friggin' guinea pig?"

Upstairs, when he took a rare break from the bar, a drape of flab hung from the bottom of his wifebeater, worn with football shorts and flip-flops. His heels cracked under so much weight and yellowed from the application of Rawleigh's Antiseptic Salve, giving him a perpetually sterile scent. *For man and beast*, it said on the tin.

One Sunday afternoon, my father evicted a trio of skinheads from the pub because a member of the gang was underage. A few hours later, I was bouncing a football around the plastic-wrapped pallets of beer. The nu-metal enthusiasts returned with reinforcements.

"Fuck you and your grandson," said one.

I was five. My father was nearly fifty. Half a dozen heavily tattooed teenagers stood on the footpath.

"Say that to my face, ya Nazis," he said, so they did.

Dad went for a quick knockout but missed, before tripping backwards on a gutter. The punks kicked the shit out of him within touching distance of me. A plasterer rushed out from the bar and punched out the ringleader.

Afterwards, we sat in the cold room waiting for the police to make a routine visit. My father applied a cool can of beer to a bleeding eye socket. I was mesmerised not by violence, but by the sight of a humiliated tough guy.

"I'd love to see them throw a punch one on one," he said. "A bunch of gutless wonders."

That year, he suffered a life-threatening heart attack. In the hospital's smoking area, my mother's hands were shaking. "What's wrong, Mum?" I asked.

"I'm worried, honey. Dad's heart is in a bad way."

I'd never set foot inside a church, but I spent the next week praying to God and negotiating Dad's entry to heaven.

"What happens after we die?" I asked Dad one day.

"Sweet stuff-all," he said. "We'll be meat for the worms."

Dad came home in a hospital bracelet, compression socks, and with fresh scars on a shaved chest. I whipped myself into panic about the fact one day he'd be dead. The interesting thing about my routine retreat into the master bedroom between midnight and sunrise is that my tough-as-nails father didn't tell me to grow some balls.

"You're a big boy now," said my mother.

But Dad pulled my small body into a stomach that just kept going, a grizzly bear harbouring a koala. "Leave him alone," he said. "He isn't doing you any harm." I knew that I'd rather cease breathing than be alive without him.

IN 1998, I WAS a six-year-old obsessed with professional wrestling and rugby league. My parents had paid $70,000 for a dilapidated worker's cottage. Firewood was piled in a dead garden bed beside the Ping-Pong table in the carport. I wasn't strong enough to lift the axe, so I watched my brothers chop kindling atop a metal plate on the concrete driveway, limbs thick with muscle.

"You don't pee sitting down, do ya?" they would enquire when I burst into tears if they didn't hand over the Super Nintendo control.

"Mummy's boy!" my sisters would sing whenever I ran to the matriarch after a disagreement on the trampoline.

"Are you a man or a mouse?" my father would ask.

"I'm a m-m-man!" I cried in my high-pitched stutter, an impediment that appeared whenever I got flustered.

At the 1998 National Rugby League grand final, I was dressed from head to toe in maroon and yellow, as the Broncos defeated the Bulldogs 38–12. Allan Langer, still captain of the Broncos, was made captain of Australia. On TV, I watched the haka—a Maori war dance—being performed by enormous Kiwis. Luckily, my father had X-ray vision for the internal organs of other men. He pointed at the biggest, meanest rival forward. "Relax," he said. "That guy's got a heart the size of a split pea."

Meanwhile, during pre-season training for the under-sevens, it became tragically apparent that the Blaine rugby league gene had gone on strike during my conception.

"You're gonna catch a cold out on the sting!" yelled my father, the team manager. "Take a run up the guts."

After winning four grand finals in seven years, Allan dramatically announced his retirement, relocating to play for a team in the north of England.

In the second season, my puppy fat was no longer adorable: I was certifiably obese, thanks to a strict diet of steak sandwiches, while the other boys were even leaner and more bloodthirsty than before.

My brother Steven carried all of my father's athletic expectations. He was the best player at St. Mary's. Dad brought his prized horseracing binoculars to Steven's games and made me magnify my brother's textbook defensive style.

"See how he creases blokes with the point of his shoulder?"

"Yeah," I said.

"No hands! Imagine they've been amputated."

The issue, in his words, was I had *shoulders like a brown snake*. I couldn't sleep before my final game of the season, visualising a boy with bleeding shoulder blades. I volunteered to warm the bench after suffering a panic attack in the locker room.

"What's wrong with ya?" asked the relieved coach, who was forced by protocol to rotate the weaker players with the best.

"I don't feel good in the guts."

"Ya got the runs?"

"Yeah."

My father knew I didn't have diarrhea, but he played along with the charade. We left before the half-time siren. He'd spent thirty years coaching rugby league players and had seen enough to know that his son wasn't one.

"Next year you should go back to playing hockey with your sisters," he said. "Don't do something unless it's fun."

At home, I flung my underwhelming body onto my bed. The anguish blared from both lungs like a full-time siren. Mum rushed in from the clothesline and hugged me. "What's the matter?" she asked.

I told her that Dad wanted me to retire from football. "I've got a heart the size of split pea," I said.

My mother tried to comfort me without betraying an underlying glee that I was more like her than my father. "Don't be silly. You've got the biggest heart of any little boy that I've ever met! It's a blessing to feel all of those feelings."

"Why can't I crease people like Steven?"

"Because you aren't Steven. You're *Lech*."

Without denying the possibility I might one day play half-back for the Brisbane Broncos, Mum explained that everyone was born with a different gift. "You've got a brain that's wider than the sky," said the stay-at-home poet, plagiarising Emily Dickinson. "It's deeper than the sea."

"I don't want a big brain. I want big guns!"

"I know, baby. But one day you'll work out that all the muscles in the world aren't worth an imagination like yours."

• • • •

QUITTING RUGBY LEAGUE heralded my improvised identity as an extroverted bookworm. On the way to cricket, my father and I ate sausage rolls smothered in tomato sauce, washed down with strawberry milk. I covered my nose with zinc and bowled leg spin off three steps like my cricketing hero Shane Warne.

"I smell b-b-blood, fellas!" I spluttered, while glowering at the puzzled batsmen like they were on death row.

On Sunday afternoons, I went to Toowoomba Library with my mother, who generally dressed in jeans and sneakers from a second-hand clothing store, where she volunteered twice a week.

"Don't sweat the small stuff, baby," said my mother, despite logging the most prosaic facts about me in a diary.

"Why do you write all that stuff?" I asked.

"Because I don't want to forget anything."

Mum preferred to write down arguments over shouting them. I grew up hearing her read other people's perfect sentences to me. And slowly but certainly I was converted to a life of reading and writing, just as she had been.

Dad sold the pub and bought the corner store across the road from my public primary school—a man who lived at high speed trying to stay alive by slowing down. It was the worst financial investment of his life. Families started fleeing the suburb due to a series of ghastly murders. The reluctant shop-keeper spent his new career bartering with junkies over the price of deep-fried food, selling *Hustler* to underage teens, and putting cigarettes on a tab for destitute pensioners.

I was delighted by the development, because we'd never spent so much uninterrupted time together. Dad studied form guides and placed bets on the horseracing, but the bets were bad more often than good. To improve his mood, I peppered him with the names of athletes and politicians from encyclo-pedias. John Curtin and Don Bradman. Martin Luther King Jr. and Muhammad Ali. Nelson Mandela and Imran Khan.

"Taking it easy's for wimps," he said.

Dad loved the Beatles, the Labor Party, and the Maroons—Queensland's rugby league team. He delivered sermons on a holy of duos that made the skin on my forearms tingle: musicians John Lennon and Paul McCartney, politicians Bob Hawke and Paul Keating, footballers Wally Lewis and Allan Langer. "They were better together," he said. "Like you and me."

But it was clear that he preferred Lennon's dark charisma over McCartney's choirboy perfectionism, Hawke's common touch over Keating's intellect, Langer's enigmatic brilliance over Lewis's persistent physicality.

"Who would ya rather have a beer with?" he asked a nine-year-old, seeking my opinion on the bygone prime ministers.

"Hawkie!"

"There's your answer."

"What was Keating like?"

Dad, that three-hundred-pound totem of masculinity, would pucker his lips and swivel his wrist in the air, insinuat-ing that Keating was a sheila. "Bloody good treasurer. But he'd rather be at the Opera House than Belmore Oval."

My father preferred doers to thinkers, loose cannons to tall poppies, larrikins to wowsers. He wanted me to be brilliant without thinking I was better than working-class men like him.

"Why did you call me *Lech*?" I asked, never getting sick of the gleam that appeared in his tired eyes.

"Lech Wałęsa is a hero. Trade unionist like your Pop. A tradesman who rewrote history. Because people believed in the rights of the worker! That's what we need, mate. A Lech Wałęsa—or a Lech *Blaine*—who stands up for the working class."

He burst into an anthem for the proletariat. *"Solidarity forever! Solidarity forever! Solidarity forever!"*

"For the union makes us strong!" I chimed in.

• • • •

THAT YEAR, 2001, Queensland's rugby league team seemed on a hiding to nothing in the State of Origin. The Maroons had lost all three matches of the previous series. They won the first game of the current series before getting flogged in the second. No halves were available for the decider.

Nobody had ever been picked from England before. But coach Wayne Bennett—whom my father called "the Svengali of Lang Park"—selected a thirty-five-year-old Allan Langer to be halfback, booking flights from the United Kingdom under a fake name.

"Shut the gates!" said Dad. "It's an old-fashioned ambush!"

Using scissors and glue, I collated every single article about the resurrection of Allan into a scrapbook. The southern media called my cousin *too unfit, too old* for the huge New South Wales forward pack.

Dad and I made a high-octane pilgrimage from the country to the state capital, blood pulsing to the drumbeat of history. On the highway, we listened to a shock jock brag about how Queensland was inferior "on paper."

"Lucky rugby league isn't played on paper, ya muppets," the driver roared into the air-conditioning vent.

I wanted to prove that life was more meaningful when captured in words, so I opened my notebook and recited a poem I'd been writing called "The Ballad of a Battler," plagiarising the cadence of "Bradman" by Paul Kelly:

history wasn't meant to star men like them
the old coach was a tall and skinny Svengali
the bald halfback was smaller than Napoleon
but he had a heart the size of Ali!

My father's eyes glinted with bewilderment and glee. He slapped the steering wheel like I'd just cracked Fermat's theorem, rendering him responsible for a genius. "You're a better poet than Banjo Paterson!"

"It's all right," I said, slightly embarrassed.

"Ya mum's son, aren't ya? More brains than brawn."

My father stopped to gamble five hundred on the underdogs to win by thirteen-plus. A payout would triple the savings in my bank account. "You hold on to it, Banjo," he said, folding and passing me the betting slip for good luck. "I'll give ya half if we get up."

At Queen Elizabeth II Stadium, the crowd was gripped by adrenaline and apprehension. With my father's horseracing binoculars, I watched maroon jerseys blow through smoke at the end of a tunnel. The two of us stood with fifty thousand others and screamed obscenely.

"The crowd to a man is standing to welcome home Allan Langer," said the commentator to those watching at home. "Former Australian captain playing his thirty-first Origin. Twenty-two test matches, 240 premiership games, and four times a grand final victor. Alfie is back in town!"

My father and I ate hot dogs and shared a carton of chips. "Feed the weak pricks!" he said.

That night, Queensland executed Bennett's game plan: bash the Blues and give the ball to Allan Langer, leading to a 40-14 thrashing of the establishment. The bald bombshell sidestepped and ducked under two huge but lumbering New South Wales forwards, planting the ball on the white line, in an act of unorthodox yet sublime physical virtuosity.

My father was mesmerised by this masterpiece, like Beethoven had been raised from the dead to play piano for Mozart, or da Vinci to paint Marilyn Monroe. Tears streamed down beaming cheeks. I'd never seen him cry.

"Jesus Christ," he said. "Alfie's got spiders on him tonight."

During the next week, while kicking my weather-damaged football, I visualised a packed stadium chanting LECH! LECH! LECH! after I led the Labor Party to an upset victory at the 2030 election. Before dinner, my father grinned at his dreamy son reading from an almanac of Australian prime ministers.

"You'll be in there one day," he said, seeing himself as having a Midas touch for greatness.

"No way," I said.

"Mate, that's what they said about Alf! Back yourself."

He had a point. A young poet's dream to be the prime minister didn't seem more implausible than my cousin becoming Queensland's greatest halfback of all time. Rationally, it was better odds. Politics didn't require innate physical greatness. I just needed to be me: a know-it-all who loved the sound of my own voice, the sight of a huge crowd, and the romance of an underdog.

• • • •

ST. MARY'S WAS WHERE sensitive young men went to become good blokes with ripped biceps and high libidos. It was a budget private school for the taciturn sons of aspirational

Catholics. My atheist father didn't have a godly ligament in his body, but he believed in tough love.

"It'll harden him up a bit," I overheard him telling my mother, who suggested I might apply for an academic scholarship at the highfalutin Grammar School.

"What difference does it make if we don't have to pay?" she asked.

"Alan Jones went to Grammar," he said. "My son isn't becoming one of them silver-spoon-fed dickheads."

On that first day at the Christian Brothers school, I made the sign of the cross for the first time and mumbled my way through the Lord's Prayer. "*Our Father, who art in heaven, hallowed be thy name...*"

I was the only class member who hadn't been baptised, which I kept secret by accepting the sacrament at Mass. Mrs. McCarthy asked me to introduce myself and tell everyone what I wanted to be when I grew up.

"I want to play for Q-Q-Queensland," I stammered.

"You'll need to lose some w-w-weight," someone whispered, to widespread laughter.

"Tell us the most interesting thing about you," said Mrs. McCarthy.

"My cousin is Alfie Langer!" I said.

This was why Nick showed me pity at morning break. His grandfather had played rugby league for St. George and cricket for New South Wales. He recruited me to sit with the football players, including Big Red, a shy, gargantuan front-rower with flaming red hair.

I followed my father's advice. "It's like jail," he'd told me that morning. "Become best mates with the biggest bloke."

• • • •

MY FATHER HAD SOLD THE SHOP and secured the lease of the Metropole Hotel for free, because it was so rundown and renowned for violence that no one else was game. His business model was to scrape up the lowest scum from a swamp. "Someone's got to take their money," he said.

A pothead Dolly Parton lookalike named Sharon hosted open mics on Friday nights and Sunday afternoons. I considered myself a Cold Chisel cover artist, studying their lyrics like Shakespeare had written them. This prepubescent Jimmy Barnes serenaded the plastered tradesmen with "Flame Trees" and "Khe Sanh."

"G'day, mate," I barked at the assembled barflies each afternoon. I played eight-ball with my tie loosened and shirt untucked until my mother arrived for dinner.

"Ya boy's a shark, Tommy," said a deadbeat regular I cleaned up. "I've never seen anything like it."

My brother John was an A-grade champion and state rep. Dad was a champion B-grader, and president of the local eight-ball and darts associations. He didn't hand out trophies for preying on blokes who couldn't shoot straight. "Pity the competition's weak as piss," he said.

On a Sunday afternoon, in the mugs' competition, I made it to the final eight before capitulating on the black ball. I shrieked and spat and threw the cue into the rack, refusing to shake my opponent's hand. My father banned me from playing eight-ball for a month.

"You need to learn how to lose like a man," he said. "I don't care how bad you choke: always shake the other bloke's hand."

This was Stoicism 101. There was no more important quality in a man than making eye contact with heartbreak.

• • • •

BY THE AGE OF ELEVEN, with the lucky country entering the seventh year of John Howard's prime ministership, I was totally beholden to a holy trinity of influences: Christianity, masculinity, and capitalism. Thanks to the mining and property booms, my parents were now technically middle-class. They went from having nothing but the lease of a rundown pub to owning six fixer-upper investment properties.

"You can't look a gift horse in the mouth," said my father, who was astounded that the bank kept offering him more mortgages at such low interest rates.

"How many do you need to be happy?" asked Mum, who objected to the basic morality of property investment.

"How long's a piece of string?" he asked.

My father assuaged his sense of class betrayal by becoming president of a virulently left-wing branch of the Labor Party, fighting for the rights of blue-collar workers and against the privatisation of state assets.

On Saturday afternoons, following cricket, we attended open houses before doing a tour of our booming rentals. It was like the scene in *The Lion King* where Mufasa shows Simba all he will inherit. Dad made a parade of the privilege he was killing himself to give me.

"Remember," he said, "one day *this* will all be yours."

My father never questioned whether *this*—a house of cards built on negative gearing and low interest rates—was something I wanted. He had all my desires for me.

Sitting in the front passenger seat, I felt protected from the threats of my father's type 2 diabetes and escalating stress. Dad left his mobile phone on silent in the glove box as a sign of love. I never felt less anxious than I did in those precious hours we spent alone together.

The rental prices outgrew the repayments, and there were only three kids left at home, so we inspected a six-bedroom home in the lower-middle-class suburb of Glenvale. *One Evergreen Court*. The bathrooms had exhaust fans and heat lamps.

"This is way too fancy for us," said my mother.

"Not anymore," said my father.

The contract settled just before Christmas 2003. I felt like the winner of *Who Wants to Be a Millionaire?* The poolroom featured a brand-new eight-ball table, with walls adorned by portraits of Allan Langer and my siblings in Queensland and Australian jerseys.

A Jacuzzi sat on the back patio. I vibrated in that gratuitous spa beside my beetroot-cheeked father. The summer breeze collected petrol fumes from the road, dog shit from the lawn, and lavender scent from clothes drying on the line.

"You wouldn't be dead for quids, would ya?" he said.

"Nah," I said. "This is living."

Mum and Dad had traded the low expectations of post-war council estates for the intolerable options of twenty-first-century suburbia. They were "cashed-up bogans," rich enough to buy a house with a dishwasher and separate rooms for the married couple, but who still looked and sounded true to their blue-collar bloodlines.

I earned my inheritance by cleaning the pub for five dollars an hour. Steven and John had turned the private quarters upstairs into a downtown bachelor pad. One morning, my dead-eyed father and I crept past bedrooms that stank of cologne, perfume, and bodily fluids. "Steve's quality over quantity," he whispered. "John's a numbers man. He'd fuck anything with a pulse, that bloke."

My brothers were apples and oranges, yet enviable in unique ways. Six-packed Steven played rugby league for the Australian university team and got high distinctions in accounting. John gave up a roofing apprenticeship to work as a bartender at the Metropole. He was a six-foot, 230-pound prop forward who punched people for fun.

"If you could get Steve's looks and John's gift of the gab with the women," said Dad, "you'd be laughing."

This didn't need to be said: my plan for adolescence was to streamline Steven's OCD perfectionism and John's self-destructive charisma into the dream son.

"What were your brothers like?" I asked.

My father and I changed kegs and cleaned the beer lines. He told me that Ted had been a boxer in the navy, George a housepainter and pugnacious rugby league star. Larrikins with quick fists and big swinging dicks.

"That's one of life's greatest mysteries," he said.

"What do you mean?"

My father wasn't too proud to admit that the two of us had been lumbered with underwhelming phalluses by comparison. "Your uncles had long massive cocks. The two of us drew the short straw."

I tried to tip crates of cans and bottles into metal drums without leaking bin juice onto my feet. The shattering glass made a cacophony with the scattering pigeons that covered the back alley in a thick layer of bird shit. I emptied ashtrays and replaced the soaked beer mats and coasters, while daydreaming about the girls I might one day fuck if I became buffer and better hung.

After emptying the slot machines, I retired to the upstairs office, where I studied my brother's porn collections. But nothing happened no matter how much I masturbated, except sharp frustration about the lack of pleasure.

At a routine flu shot, I raised the issue with Dr. Rattray, the family GP. I didn't know that he'd just prescribed Lexapro to my mother for the bouts of unhappiness that had followed her blossoming prosperity like hay fever.

The doctor pulled my foreskin back with gloved fingers and gave a shy cock his unconvincing tick of approval.

"This is actually just about average," he said. "Unfortunately, the boys with the median penises aren't the ones flashing them."

"Is there anything else I can do?" I asked.

"Well, you could lose a little weight. You're still a bit heavy at the moment. And that's not doing you any favours when you look in the bathroom mirror."

I went on a detox from meat pies, steak sandwiches, and soft drinks, subsisting on low-sugar cereal for breakfast, a green apple for morning tea, and rice cakes and tinned tuna for lunch.

I supplemented my diet with a summer fitness kick. My sister Hannah—captain of the Queensland hockey team—aspired to Olympic gold. "You need to do burpees while everyone else is sunbaking," she said.

We spent Boxing Day on a brutal boot camp in the front yard. I did push-ups and sit-ups in the scorching summer sun, and hill sprints with my neck and arms poked through a garbage bag, like a jockey before final weigh-in.

"You've been training the house down," said Dad, nose burnt from lawn bowls. "I can barely recognise ya!"

"I don't love you any more or less than before," said my mother, but I'd stopped paying her much attention.

My mediocre rugby league career was to peak at the age of twelve. Our coach, Mr. Manthey, was the same age as Allan Langer, but the schoolboy prodigy had never cracked first grade at the Brisbane Broncos due to four straight knee reconstructions. "It's a shame," he told me. "I was never the same player."

I was determined to make the St. Mary's under-twelve As. My tear ducts had been plugged and the stutter was gone. Unfortunately, I still had the size of a halfback and the speed of a slow front-rower. But I had a secret weapon at the trials: my best mate Big Red. The star player let the class clown repeatedly upend him defensively, while moaning like I'd pierced his spleen.

"Lech Blaine!" said Mr. Manthey. "That's textbook defence."

On Monday morning, my name was the final entry on the noticeboard. *17: Lech Blaine.* Mr. Manthey was the first coach to glimpse my true abilities: thanks to thousands of hours watching games, I processed the plays in slow motion, divining tactics and outcomes.

"I don't need you to be Big Red or Nick," he said. "I want you to come onto the field, make your tackles and tell the team what you *see* three sets ahead."

There was another benefit of my rope-a-dope approach to suffering physical punishment: watching the benchwarmer get folded like a card table a few times fired up the genuine super-stars like Big Red and Nick.

"Always take the next hit-up after Big Red," said Dad. "That kid's a unit! You'll be like a cyclist in a slipstream."

In the statewide quarterfinals, we played at the sacred North Ipswich Reserve, where Allan Langer had debuted for the Ipswich Jets at seventeen. I savoured the smell of strapping tape and muscle cream, the taste of Gatorade in a plastic mouthguard, the scrape of Steeden headgear.

My father's arms were folded over a puffy chest. "They can't run without legs!" he shouted in a foghorn voice.

It's hard to distil the beauty and brutality of rugby league. A potential black hole sat waiting at the end of each tackle. I played through a fractured finger, before coming off on suspicion of a concussion, with a black eye from a stray boot. But for once my job was done.

"Players' player goes to Lech Blaine," said Mr. Manthey in the locker room, where I led the victory song of "When the Saints Go Marching In." My face and body throbbed, but group approval was the greatest painkiller of all.

"You had an absolute blinder, mate," said my father.

Football was about drama and adrenaline, karma, and kinship. I chased the basic belonging of a male body racing through space towards adoration and oblivion.

FOR MY THIRTEENTH BIRTHDAY, Dad organised a private dinner at Hog's Breath Cafe. "Two rib fillets," he said to the waitress with a wink. "Medium rare, Diane sauce."

Embarrassed by my dramatic weight loss, Dad had joined a gym and lost forty pounds. "Train hard," he said. "But play harder."

Dad illustrated the difference between illicit drugs and the garden-variety vices that paid for my private-school fees by topping up my Diet Coke with his Scotch.

"Marijuana will give ya schizophrenia," he whispered.

"I'm not gonna be some druggo!" I said.

"How about you swear on your mum's life," he said, so we shook hands on my fidelity to binge drinking.

During the summer holidays, when the pub doors were locked and the bartender was counting the tills, he slipped me a fifty to deposit into whichever slot machine was overdue to pay out. The logbook of major jackpot winners was filled with his creative aliases.

"Five-dollar spins," he said. "It's the only way to win."

My record-breaking collection was on a horseracing-themed machine called Spring Carnival. Pleasure lit up between my brain cells like a fireworks display. I wished that the free games and hypnotic jingles never finished.

"You little beaut-*ay*!" my father sang.

I started high school sporting a hairstyle known as the St. Mary's bird's nest, mix of mohawk and mullet. Tim had a matching haircut, except without my rat's tail. His parents were Catholics from working-class stock. We became best friends in the intense way of young men allocating their preferences within a vast marketplace.

"That ratty is filthy," he said. "I respect it."

"It's part of my religious beliefs."

"Boganism?"

Before we got our ID photos taken, the assistant principal ruthlessly amputated my rat's tail with scissors from the science lab. It was a bad omen. My hard-fought status as a jock was short-lived. I had a hundred fresh potential contenders, and most of them had spent the summer profiting from puberty.

"Hey, pretty boy," shouted Mr. Canning, who'd coached Steven at the height of his schoolboy stardom. "Didn't your brother teach you how to hit with your shoulders?"

After the trials, my name was recited in the Cs rather than the As with Big Red, Nick, and Tim. I ambushed Mr. Canning outside his office. "I had a bad day," I said. "I just need another go."

"Look," he said. "You've got great ball skills. But you're slower than a stoned snail."

At the end of that season, I decided to retire from rugby league, a jaded, failed athlete at thirteen. I directed all of my sports ambitions into eight-ball. My father and I entered a team with two Papua New Guineans from the slaughterhouse.

My anti-marijuana father would drive home after drinking eight or nine Scotch and Cokes in a white Ford Falcon pickup with red personalised number plates: TOM. "I'm sober as a judge," he'd say.

The grand final was on home turf at the Metropole. I secretly slipped half a nip of vodka into my orange juice as a nerve relaxant. Liquor made a worryguts unbeatable.

Dad—the team captain—nominated me for the tiebreaker. I fell behind off the break but clawed back onto the black. The opponent snookered me. I chalked the tip of the cue three times and hit the white ball on the top right to make it spin left off the cush. The white skewed through a thin slit past two smalls. The black dropped in the hole and filled the chip in my soul.

"Go you good thing!" said Dad, clapping theatrically.

My father dropped me off for a sleepover at Big Red's farm. I swigged from a triumphant stubbie of beer. "Nothin' tastes better than winner's piss," he grinned.

Unbeknownst to him, my supervised consumption of alcohol was only a matinee: Big Red's older brother Terry was having a party for the first football team. I had stashed a bottle of Bundaberg rum and a packet of Winfield Blue cigarettes in my backpack while cleaning the pub.

Big Red and I set up a tent in a paddock. We mixed the rum with ginger ale and infiltrated the party as soon as it was too dark for Red's parents to see us.

Around the bonfire, seniors toasted the novelty of a chain-smoking thirteen-year-old who sculled beer like Bob Hawke. "Come on, the blue and the white!" I shouted, before crushing a tin of lager down my gullet.

At dawn, I awoke on a haybale, half my eyebrow gone thanks to a Gillette razor. Unwisely, I decided to lose the surviving eyebrow before my father's arrival. "Did you try to fuck a lawn mower?" he asked.

The following Saturday, I attended the Toowoomba eight-ball banquet at Rumours, a local function centre. My father, as president of the association, pressed the flesh with his bickering constituents while my shit-faced teammates supplied a minor with cans of bourbon and cola.

"It's one of my proudest moments," Dad said, in a post-dinner address, "to win a grand final with my young bloke."

After collecting the premiership trophy, I betrayed my inebriation by slurring "Eagle Rock" in karaoke, dropping my trousers during the chorus like I'd seen so many drunks do. The room hooted with amusement at the coronation of a precocious rogue. Then I regurgitated five cans of bourbon across the stage.

The level of outrage from onlookers correlated closely with whether or not they belonged to the rival clique counting the numbers against the president.

"Don't tell your mother" was all that my hungover father said the next day. "Or she'll skin the both of us."

On Monday morning, the sports section of the local paper featured a leak from one of Dad's anonymous rivals, alleging that he had allowed underage drinking at the banquet. Dad immediately lodged his resignation.

My mother didn't need an investigation to guess the identity of the legless adolescent. "I don't want my son to be known as the town drunk," she said.

"Maybe he wouldn't drink so much if you weren't half-sloshed most nights," said my father.

"Thomas, don't you *dare* make this about *my* drinking," Mum screeched tearfully. "You let him get away with murder. And one day he's going to get hurt."

• • • •

I WAS OFFICIALLY GROUNDED, and spent a rainless wet season working in the liquor store of the Bernborough Tavern, Dad's most profitable business yet. It was named after a famous dead racehorse and situated on the main strip of Oakey, a town in the guts of redneck country. My job was to restack cartons using the forklift and wrap beer bottles in newspaper to help keep them refrigerated.

On the daily pilgrimage between the suburbs and the bush, hurtling past drought-stricken farm paddocks, my increasingly reclusive mother complained about being treated as a chauffeur for the teenage employee of a husband she rarely saw anymore. "I'm just a cog in his machine," she said, "until he doesn't need me."

I plugged in headphones and muted her gripes with the iPod paid for by her adversary. Steven's Nirvana and Pearl Jam mixtapes provided a segue to the Pixies, the Stooges, and the Smiths. I wrote down couplets in a notepad and imagined myself singing them with the same sexual tension as Morrissey or Iggy Pop.

This musical awakening coincided with my breakthrough ejaculation. *My God!* I finally understood what all the fuss was about. The junior liquor shop attendant spent every spare moment in the cold room with *People* magazine while jerking off into one of the brown paper bags that we used for wine bottles.

"You're gonna get frostbite in there," said my father when he came downstairs from the front bar.

"It's too hot out here," I said.

The hardest part of the job was asking for proof of age from abattoir workers, whose Southern Cross tattoos matched their xenophobic "Love It or Leave It" bumper stickers.

"Suck my dick, ya unborn-lookin' little cunt!" said one customer, in reference to my vandalised eyebrows.

It was the unforgettable summer of the Cronulla race riots. I was the closest source of beer and rum cans, as Alan Jones—a right-wing shock jock—whipped the local neo-Nazis into a frenzy.

"I'll tell you what they should do," said one deadbeat regular. "Round all these shitskins up and drown 'em."

"You're a Nazi!" I said.

"You're a poofter," he spat.

Each day, the clearest dissenting voice of compassion was a refugee advocate named Ian Rintoul, who defended boat people on the news. I tracked down his Hotmail address, and we became pen pals. Rintoul sent reams of socialist magazines featuring diatribes against the Iraq War and offshore detention.

"There's no difference between Labor and Liberal," I said to my father on the way home one night.

"That's real easy to say," he said, aghast at my rising nihilism. "You've never worked a hard day in your life."

My identity crisis continued into the new school year. Now that my sports career was over, I defected from the jocks to a motley crew of musicians and drama students, ignoring pleas from Big Red, Nick, and Tim to remain faithful.

Most controversially from my father's perspective, I registered a moral opposition to horseracing. "It's quite inhumane," I said, when he asked if I wanted to come watch one of his new thoroughbreds run.

"*Inhumane*. I'll tell ya what's inhumane—thinking everyone's an inbred 'cept for you. Wake up to yourself."

That year, 2006, the culture war between us engulfed the whole district. As dams edged towards empty, the mayor—an environmentalist named Dianne Thorley—tried to introduce recycled sewage water. Due to her short hair and a gruff voice, she was accused of being a lesbian. Clive Berghofer, a real estate developer, joined forces with Lyle Shelton, a Pentecostal on council. Their slogan was simple: *IT'S OKAY TO VOTE NO*.

"We are known as the Garden City," said Berghofer, a high-school dropout who'd subdivided ten thousand blocks of land. "Now we are the Shit City or Poowoomba."

After the release of *An Inconvenient Truth*, which I watched with self-righteousness, 62 per cent of my hometown voted no to recycled water based on fake news funded by a megalomaniac millionaire. Capitalism and Christianity waged a scatological battle against science.

I can't wait to escape this place, I wrote to Rintoul.

• • • •

THAT SUMMER, I returned to the liquor shop a different boy from the one of the Christmas before. On a Sunday afternoon, "This Charming Man" by the Smiths jangled as I served a farmer, who suffered an anaphylactic reaction.

"Are you one of those faggots?" he asked.

Mercifully, the door to the front bar swung open, revealing my brother John. "What's goin' on?" he asked, detecting the tension from the customer's disgusted lips and the attendant's blushing cheeks.

"He called me a faggot," I said.

"Why don't you call *me* a faggot," John said, before landing a clean punch on the customer's chin. "Ya faggot!"

A feeling of safety and shame followed the quarrel. Did my reliance on John's muscle make me any better than the bigot? "Thanks, mate," I said.

Morrissey kept whining. John slapped the laptop shut like it contained a virus, and put my pink-tipped copy of Plath's *The Bell Jar* in the drawer with the porn magazines. "Cut that shit out around here," he said.

I didn't think that I was gay, but had faced persistent suspicions about this possibility since growing my hair long and carrying a book with me everywhere.

My mother had recently brought home a second-hand hardcover called *Treasury of Great Short Stories*. "So that was the end of that marriage," read the final sentence of an eight-page masterpiece by Virginia Woolf.

Hemingway bored me, but I loved Fitzgerald, because he allowed the kinds of emotions that I'd learned to repress to erupt above the surface. Joyce's "The Dead" led me to *A Portrait of the Artist as a Young Man*, which I borrowed from Toowoomba Library. In the liquor shop, I suffered the rapture of having my specific alienation captured by an Irish stranger ninety years earlier.

My Grade Ten English teacher, Mr. Shaw, was a wisp of a man with a feminine inflection. He suggested that I enter a statewide writing competition. I won with a short story about a woman who dreams of murdering her father, the philandering prime minister.

"This isn't a little hobby," he said conspiratorially in the hallway after school. "A university degree in literature and writing could turn you into something special."

I had sixteen aunties and uncles, and ten of them hadn't made it past primary school. Only one had reached Grade Ten.

To compensate, my father wanted me to study something magnificent like law or economics.

At the halfway mark of Grade Ten, on the way home from a careers seminar with my feuding parents, I announced that I intended to study English literature.

"That's exactly what I would have done!" said Mum. "Don't worry about money. Do what you love."

In the rear-view mirror, a king saw his legacy disappearing. He was appalled that I was becoming a nervous bookworm who preferred creativity and solitude to popularity and profit. In other words, my mother's son.

"I thought you wanted to be the PM," he said.

"You can't just *be* the prime minister."

Dad didn't believe that I needed to literally be prime minister, but that I was raising a white flag to my enemies by not wanting to participate in the political process. "There's no point pissing in from outside the tent."

The 2007 federal election provided us with an opportunity to reconcile. We handed out how-to-vote cards for Labor at one of the most right-wing polling booths in the country. "Your face will be on the signs one day," said my father, trying to reignite my political ambitions.

That night, I wore a Che Guevara T-shirt and red Converse to dinner with John and Dad. Dad proposed a toast during the cheese-bread entrée. "To Mr. Howard," he said. "Suck shit, dickhead."

John was only twenty-four, but he had three daughters and a mortgage. He was my father's second-in-charge at the family business, and belonged to a new generation of working-class conservatives.

"Kevin Rudd will fuck this country," he said, referring to the newly elected Labor prime minister. "You may as well open the floodgates to boat people."

"You sound like a redneck," I said.

John's feelings came from his mouth in a stream, and I could tell that he'd been dwelling on them. "Do-gooders like you are ruining this country," he said. "Everyone's a racist nowadays. And it'll be people like me with real jobs who pay for all the damage. While smug cunts like you are jerking each other off at university."

I tried to hold back the tears that welled in my eyes whenever I got into a fight with the men in my family.

"*Solidarity forever!*" my father sang, aiming to inflame John, or to induce a truce between the two of us. But I knew he had more in common with his tough bartender son than with me.

"For the union makes us strong," I whispered.

Deep down, the only people I felt solidarity with were my favourite musicians and writers. I wanted to be an artist, not a son, brother, mate, Australian, *larrikin*. But in the dusk of a right-wing dynasty, my dreams felt like treason.

Blank
Volcanoes

I CAME OF AGE on the grave of a volcano. There was no saving me from the flames.

By December 2007, Hannah had graduated and hightailed it to Brisbane. Trent was on a fishing trawler somewhere. Rebecca and Steven had moved interstate. John lived five minutes away, with his own family.

"I'll have too much time on my hands," said Mum.

Summer was the season for people to stop playing dumb. Before Christmas, my father announced that he was moving out too. The s-word was never mentioned, let alone the petrifying d-word. "Your mum and me are taking a breather," was all Dad said.

"You're splitting the sheets?" I asked.

"Let's just take this one week at a time."

Dad left everything except the pickup, a suitcase of clothes, and fifty items of sports memorabilia. He moved into the private quarters of the Drayton Tavern, a rundown pub in a rough suburb.

"You can't take it to the grave," my mother cried during the rumpus-room debates about their doomed marriage.

Dying with an intact modest property empire was precisely what my father had in mind. Fresh from a triple heart bypass, he offered his wife a debtless family home in exchange for all the rental properties and bank repayments. He was terrified of having a final, fatal heart attack and my inheritance getting squandered.

"She's a great lady, ya mum," he said. "Such a shame. I wish it could be different. She's a bloody good woman."

I interpreted his leaving as a vote of no confidence in me, and decided I wanted to be prime minister again.

That summer, I spent every spare moment at Tim's nuclear household in Middle Ridge, with parents who didn't seem sick of their son. His friendship was the only safe bet in a life filled with flakes. At night, we binged on slapstick comedies, before sunburnt days playing backyard cricket and one-on-one football.

"You're a prop trapped in a halfback's body," he said.

I convinced Tim to stay at St. Mary's until graduation, rather than dropping out to finish his bricklaying apprenticeship. In return, I defected back to sit with the rugby league players on the first day of Grade Eleven. "Penis!" we shouted, until the loudest got sent to the Responsible Thinking Classroom for detention.

The class chameleon went on holidays as a sarcastic artist and came back as a sensitive new-age jock. I tried to plug the round hole of my father's departure and my mother's depression with the square peg of high-school popularity.

After Dad left, Mum's weekly carton of Bundaberg Rum & Cola became a daily six-pack. A foster carer whose love for troubled children had won official recognition from the government could now barely make eye contact with her only biological child. "My arthritis gets bad in the afternoons," she said, asking if I could get lifts home from school.

Eventually, I called bullshit on her continued excuses, sending an email from my laptop in the self-contained granny flat to the desktop computer in the poolroom.

Mum, it is time to talk about your drinking. You are a different woman to the one who I loved growing up. I'm no longer receiving an adequate standard of parenting.

I was gripped by the delusion that her drinking drove my father away, rather than the more convoluted truth that she drank to pacify anxiety about the psychological titanic of their marriage. The final paragraph of my ultimatum was an olive branch shot from a cannon.

We need to work together to make things better, because I don't want to remember you as an alcoholic.

Mum never responded to or mentioned the email. We skirted each other with expertise. When we did cross paths, I detailed my father's complaints to fresh effect; Mum shrank away in tears. I slunk off to the granny flat. She felt betrayed. I was bitter that her nervous breakdown had been reserved for me.

• • • •

ON A SATURDAY AFTERNOON, I went to watch Tim, Nick, and Big Red play for the Souths Tigers, my old team.

"DEEE-FENCE!" chanted a father. "DEEE-FENCE!"

Nick had left St. Mary's for Downlands at the start of that year. I sat on the sidelines with Henry and Dom, two of Nick's fresh connections, as my dependable friend scored an impressive three tries.

"Are you coming to the afterparty, Blaine Train?" asked Henry, offering a nickname like we'd known each other since preschool.

"I don't want to start a fight," I said.

There was a history of brawls between Downlands and St. Mary's boys at parties and socials. St. Mary's were generally the gatecrashers and instigators. But for once, my absence of muscles was an advantage.

"You're coming," snickered Henry. "Pre-drinks are at Nick's."

I'd been planning to attend a St. Mary's gathering with the same old faces. But a shindig at a mansion with my new mates, plus another hundred strangers, was irresistible.

"I just got my licence," said Dom. "Get a lift with us."

After the game, I got into the people-mover belonging to Dom's parents, beside a bruised Nick. He had no issue with me riding the coattails of his social prestige.

"I love you, Blainey," he said. "Shit, you're funny."

50 Cent's "In Da Club" blasted from the speakers, segueing into "Lollipop" by Lil Wayne. A revving engine and a carful of laughter was a panacea for my sense of rejection.

. . . .

IN THE SUMMER THAT FOLLOWED, I spent every spare moment at Nick's expanding McMansion in Toowoomba's northwestern sprawl. His truck mechanic father had added a bedroom, a bar, a rumpus room, and a pool since I had first stayed over as a wowed ten-year-old. It was now a halfway house for private-school students on holidays.

come over right now, Nick messaged me. *hurry up!!!!!!*

I arrived with a carton of cheap beers and watched Nick and Henry finish a gym workout in the home cinema.

"Do you feel the burn?" asked Nick.

"I feel it!" said Henry. "God, I feel the burn."

Henry was a smash hit with the opposite sex.

"Give me your six-pack," I said, "and I'd be unstoppable."

"You don't need a six-pack if you have a personality," he said. "Girls want someone who can talk to them."

"Are you the love guru?"

"Listen to the man," said Nick, whose biceps were the size of my thighs. "Henry is friends with all the birds."

Nick and Henry switched places on the bench press.

"The Blaine Train is the most eligible bachelor in Too-woomba," said Henry. "He just hasn't worked it out yet."

Dom arrived after dusk in an eight-seat van packed with a motley crew. Will was there, a loyal attendee of these last-minute jamborees. So was Vincent. Because his blond hair was cut in a daringly metrosexual style, and he was in the choir and school musicals, some of the jocks called him a *faggot* behind his back.

"It's good," said Nick, who'd found a different tribe. "We're not just a bunch of dumb pricks."

A man pulled into the driveway, a deer in the headlights, freeing his daughter and a group of her friends.

"Yes, Dad!" she said. "I won't get pregnant."

Beer pong distracted twenty teenagers from a mosquito ambush. "A-Punk" by Vampire Weekend segued into "Electric Feel" by MGMT. Henry flirted with Eliza, a tall blonde. She went to an elite girls' school filled with sophisticated students who didn't usually associate with St. Mary's boys. Tongue-tied, I went inside to play eight-ball with one of the guys.

Henry took my arm. "This is Frida," he said, leading me to one of Eliza's friends. "She's the only person here smarter than you."

Frida was olive-skinned with a billowing brunette bun. She had a small face that was symmetrical except for a mole high on the right cheek. I'd never seen jean shorts and a black crop top worn with such sangfroid.

"I've heard a lot about you," she said.

"What? From who?"

"Henry. I came prepared for a debate."

Dentists had altered Frida's teeth to perfection, but her gaze was naturally amazing. Brown irises were guarded by thick black eyebrows. Her father was from a well-known Lebanese family who grew rich in a new country.

"I have a question," she said. "Don't be offended."

"Go for it."

"What the hell is *Lech* short for?"

"Nothing. I'm named after Lech Wałęsa."

"Who's he?"

I stared at Frida in mock horror. "The old Polish president? Leader of the Solidarity movement. Winner of the 1983 Nobel Peace Prize. I thought you were meant to be a genius!"

"He sounds like a top bloke. But we haven't done Eastern Europe in Modern History yet. Ask me about Vietnam."

We sparred about the pros and cons of Ho Chi Minh. Then Frida jabbed back, "I, too, was named after a famous person."

I tried to think of well-known Fridas, but came up blank.

"Frida Kahlo!" she said. "My mother was an artist."

"Never heard of her," I said.

"Aren't you interested in art?" she asked.

"I look at the paintings," I said, "but nothing happens. I reckon painters beat around the bush too much."

Frida snickered. "Like politicians?"

"Politics is real. Even if the leaders are full of shit."

Henry and Eliza collected us on their way upstairs, followed by Vincent and a brunette named Anna.

"Talking about politics!" said Anna. "You were meant to be."

On the front balcony, we shared a cigarette among five—Vincent didn't smoke—and swigged from a bottle of Jacob's Creek chardonnay that Eliza was holding.

"Let's play spin the bottle," said Anna.

We retreated to a bedroom. Vincent's spin landed on Anna. They kissed in the dimness. It was Frida's turn next. She pointed the bottle directly at me, like a compass.

"We'll leave you guys to it," said Eliza, before she and Henry relocated to the balcony. Vincent and Anna took the hint and moved to the spare bedroom next door.

Frida and I kissed quickly and then slowly, slowly and then quickly, quickly and then slowly. My head spun with the information of straight teeth and wayward fingers.

"I have a confession to make," said Frida.

"You have herpes? I knew it."

"No! I stalked your Myspace when Henry told me about you. And you might be the only person I know who likes Pavement."

"Is that a good thing?" I asked.

"That's *why* I'm making out with you."

Our tryst was interrupted by a car horn. A minute later, a ringtone sounded through the wall. A minute more, and Anna banged on the door. "My father is here!" she yelled. "Sorry, Frida. I told him not to come till eleven."

Frida kissed me insistently. "Text me," she said. "Get my number from Henry."

Eliza, Anna, and Frida disappeared downstairs. The chauffeur beeped again. Through the curtains, I watched three apparitions slide into a luxury four-wheel drive.

Henry entered the bedroom and put an arm around me. "See, Blaine Train," he said. "Girls dig personality."

My lips made a big, dumb grin. We got two beers from the fridge and went back outside to the lingering party.

• • • •

AT THE END OF FIRST TERM, Nick travelled to New Zealand and Fiji on a prestigious school rugby union tour. I drove from St. Mary's to Downlands to collect Henry, who had narrowly missed out on team selection. He couldn't keep his dejection a secret from me.

"No offence," he said. "But I wish I was in Fiji."

For the first time, he stayed the night at my noticeably broken home. We watched *Billy Madison* in the granny flat. Henry was well-mannered to my mother and didn't cringe at the sunken couches or frayed carpet, but couldn't ignore the outlines of missing memorabilia.

"Did your old man move out?" he asked.

"Yep."

"When?"

I opened the sliding door and lit a cigarette. The collar of our half-breed dalmatian, Mazda, rattled as he licked my feet.

"The end of 2007."

"Christ," he said, joining me. "You never said anything."

I could talk to Henry, perhaps because his parents had divorced when he was young. We had kindred sensitivities. I witnessed his frequent moments of empathy and longing, a hint that he wished reality might be different.

"That sucks," he said. Henry talked about his parents' divorce without bitterness or self-pity, which made me feel less damaged. "Remember not to take it personally."

On Saturday afternoon, Henry and I picked up Tim and Big Red on the way to the gathering at Dom's newly built house in Mount Lofty, where Will and Vincent had stayed the night before. Dom's parents were away.

"You Downlands guys are actually all right," said Tim.

We strawpedoed Vodka Cruisers overlooking the pool. A koala sanctuary shared the horizon with a rifle range.

"You should see what Frida is doing," said Henry.

"I don't think she's keen on me," I said.

Since we made out at Nick's place, Frida kept rain-checking our first date, blaming pedantic parents.

"Dude," said Henry. "She likes you."

So I texted Frida to see what she was doing.

you're in luck Mr. Walesa, she texted back.

She arrived in a taxi with Eliza and Anna. "Happy crucifixion, Jesus!" Frida announced.

After a game of Never Have I Ever, we sauntered from a fog-swamped Mount Lofty to Queens Park for the Australian Gospel Music Festival, trespassing through Downlands. There was a grim history of boarders hanging themselves from the camphor laurels.

My friends tried to convince me that the spirits of dead students haunted the heritage-listed buildings.

"Tell me none of you believe in that shit," I said.

"Don't disrespect the fuckin' ghosts!" said Will. "They're listening..."

Henry lit up his face with a phone. In a rasping voice, he told a story about a teacher on fire often seen running through the trees towards the highway.

"True story," he said. "I've seen him."

"You're a liar!" cried Frida, linking her fingers with mine.

We reached the footpath at the front of a rambling campus. Frida and I fell back from the others. She used the privacy to compare her grades with mine. I sat on a perfect score in English literature—100 per cent—five rungs better than Frida, who was viscerally wounded by the defeat. She was a prefect of unique beauty and conventional perfectionism.

"Who do you want to be when you grow up?" I asked, not *what*, an appropriate faux pas.

"I want to shake up classical music," she said. "Like Philip Glass."

"Philip who?" I asked.

"*Glass.* The composer and pianist. You know so many big words, Mr. Blaine. But deep down you're still a philistine."

Frida's parents wanted her to study at the Conservatorium, but she remained undecided about the practicality of piano in the face of rising sea levels and Israeli occupations of Palestine.

"Anyhoo. That's a little bit about the adversity of being Frida. Tell me about Lech Blaine. Who do *you* want to be?"

Much of my untamed youth had been spent translating speech into plainer language, or blunting my sense of fraudulence with alcohol. Now I was overcome by the pleasure of speaking to another person in the native tongue of my internal monologue.

"I want to write the Great Australian Novel," I said, "or be the prime minister. It changes depending on the day."

"You can't be an artist *and* a politician."

"Why not?"

"Popularity is the enemy of art."

I explained how I grew up idolising prime ministers Bob Hawke and Paul Keating, before growing disillusioned with the Labor Party's basically patriotic embrace of capitalism. But I became equally afraid that my political purity was the opposite of obtaining power.

"What made you fear that?"

"I had a Road to Damascus moment," I said, alluding to my series of debates with John about asylum seekers.

Frida's eyes crinkled with pleasure. I wanted to make her cry with laughter like my life depended on it. *That sound!* It was the opposite of sorrow.

"I never thought I'd hear a guy in Toowoomba describe himself as having a Road to Damascus moment."

"Sorry," I said. "I don't usually talk like this."

"This is the best conversation of my life," she said.

I kissed her impulsively on the lips. Neither of us blinked. Frida squeezed my fingers. "You're an excellent person," she said, as if a little surprised by this. "It's so nice knowing you."

• • • •

THE MAY LONG WEEKEND started fast and lasted forever. I wiped sleep from my eyes and swiped for new texts. Frida had kept in consistent contact since Easter Saturday. The next afternoon, I was taking her to the movies, before a party at Vincent's place.

In the car, I played a Philip Glass CD while picking up Nick, unusually tanned from the Fijian rugby union tour.

"What is this?" he asked.

"Nothing," I said, switching to an alternative rock station.

We drove half an hour to Tim's place in Middle Ridge. "My brothers!" said Tim. "Buckle up for a big one."

Nick bought banana bread on the way to Downlands. "I'm carb loading," he said. The back seat was a potpourri of petrol, overripe fruit, and heavy aerosol deodorant.

"You better axe someone today," said Tim.

The Downlands First XV were playing a Brisbane school. The main oval attracted a flock of students staring sternly at perfect turf steamrolled into steep terrain.

"*Oh, when the Saints...*" I hummed.

We watched Dom and Hamish play in the Thirds, Henry in the Seconds and Nick in the Firsts. Tim and I, two St. Mary's boys, withstood the quizzical looks of strangers as we hung in the stands with Dom, unofficial team photographer, and Hamish, who helped lead the chants.

"Oi, Henry!" screamed Hamish, as Henry sat on the bench in his cherished Firsts jersey. "*Oi!* Henry."

When Henry turned around, Dom captured his shy mixture of pride and vulnerability on film.

"Fire up, Downlands," shouted the crowd. "Fire up, Downlands, fire up!"

After an upset victory by Downlands, Henry invited five of us to a barbeque at his place. Hamish was staying at Dom's. They left to get ready. Tim, Nick, and Henry piled into my car, so that I could take it home.

Hannah bought us a carton of cheap beers and dropped us at Henry's place in Highfields. At the end of a winding driveway, a brand-new manor cradled the landscape. Henry's stepfather was a successful builder.

"Let me know if you need a lift," said Hannah.

Henry delivered a tour of the residence. The paint and carpet smelled fresh, offset by designer furniture. Walls were decorated with art and family portraits.

"Welcome to my crib," said Henry.

"This place is legit," said Tim.

I suffered an involuntary vision of my mum drinking alone in a room cluttered with pictures of a missing husband and children, and my father cheerfully pouring beers at a clubhouse for recreational racists.

"Yep," I said. "This is amazing."

"It goes all right," said Henry.

We met Melissa, Henry's elegantly dressed mother. "You are all more than welcome to stay over," she said, and this seemed the likeliest option. I was saving my gunpowder for Sunday night.

Dom and Hamish arrived. Dom had just bought a gold Ford Fairlane, meaning that we no longer had access to the eight-seat people-mover.

"I'm gonna miss the van," said Nick.

Henry's driving test was still months away. He did an inspection of his panel van, which needed a motor, four wheels, and a fresh coat. Hamish and Dom went to collect kindling for the fireplace from the jungle out the front.

"D'you wanna start the fire, Blainey?" Hamish asked me.

"I wouldn't have a clue," I said.

"You're supposed to be from the bush," said Dom.

"I grew up in a pub," I said, "not on a farm."

The six of us sat around a table sipping mid-strength beers and shivering until the miniature bonfire heated up, while Henry's stepdad supervised and cooked a barbeque.

"Get some pictures," said Henry.

I took a few on my digital camera—Henry pouting while Hamish smiled, Dom and Nick grinning, Tim grimacing, he and I scowling through the smoke.

Henry's stepfather retired upstairs. Will arrived in a small car with three girls. It changed the atmosphere. Henry and Nick were in their element. Hamish and I grew quieter. We went out the front for a smoke.

"I haven't been to Wondai in yonks," I said.

"Come out to the farm in the holidays," he said.

Hamish told me that he wanted to study engineering in Brisbane after school, a destiny overlapping with mine and Henry's. This seemed like fate. We returned to the warmth of the courtyard with a new rapport.

Someone received a text message from the friend of a friend with the address of a party near the airport. It didn't matter whether the event actually existed: as soon as there was an exit strategy, leaving became a hypnotic possibility. Ten bodies split between two cars.

The girls were noncommittal. I wanted to stay at Henry's, because I had my rendezvous with Frida planned for the next day and didn't want a hangover.

We came to a vague plan: Dom would drive back to his place. Those who wanted to go to the party could make their own way. Those who weren't keen could go home. The plan relied on the arithmetic that the female driver would chauffeur two of the guys to Dom's.

"Let's get going," said Dom.

Henry went upstairs to kiss his mother goodbye. We skylarked around the Honda Civic parked in the driveway. I smoke-bombed from the posse to claim the front passenger seat, gripping my iPhone like an asthma puffer.

are you getting crunk tonight?? asked Frida.

nah! i'm a mature old man these days

Footsteps came towards the getaway vehicle. There'd been a shift in the plan. The girls were driving the other way and needed to make it home by curfew, so seven bodies now divided into five seats. Doors were slammed. Tim took the middle, Henry on his left and Will on his right.

Nick and Hamish arrived last. I didn't see the process of their entry. Teenage boys don't stage committee meetings before climbing into trunks. And that's how we wound up in a car on the dark edge of town.

The Graduate

"Well, everyone can master a grief but he that has it."
WILLIAM SHAKESPEARE

Class
Excursions

RETURNED TO SCHOOL on a Monday morning, sixteen days after the collision. Leadership badges were pinned to my navy tie. On the way, I drove past garbage trucks with robotic limbs emptying wheelie bins. Sandwich boards advertised bags of THE PUREST THOROUGHBRED MANURE IN TOOWOOMBA. This was the most shocking thing about trauma: the continuing ordinariness of a world invisibly rigged against me.

I didn't shiver or burst any hidden rivers of emotion as I accelerated past the garage two hundred yards from my school, where two metal relics from the crash were padlocked inside chain-link cages, so police could study them.

At school, my mates bag-whacked each other and threw apples at the younger kids. I kept getting tugged from the present to the past by an undertow of sorrow.

At 3:15 PM, I lit a cigarette and drove from the student car park to the police station for my first interrogation. For the previous fortnight, Toowoomba had been rife with innuendo. The fictions filtered back, mostly through my father, the pub owner, a profession second only to taxi drivers when it came to gauging the deranged population. Drunken customers leaked the rumours that friends didn't want to upset me with. *Don't shoot the messenger, but* ...

The driver was speeding, clearly. At some point he'd been blindfolded from behind. The front passenger—me—had yanked on the steering wheel. We were committed to a suicide pact. Witnesses saw ziplock bags of weed on the back seat. In certain retellings, pot became speed or crystal meth. Bongs and pipes littered the back seat. At the hospital, every illegal substance imaginable had been located in the driver's bloodstream.

Sources were untraceable. Someone's sister played golf with the wife of a nurse from the hospital. Another person's brother rode motorbikes with a detective.

Rumours bloomed into truth. White lies became facts. The simplest explanation—that generally law-abiding teenagers made a rash decision to overload a car, before their sober driver overshot a bend while under the speed limit—was the only version considered implausible.

The senior constable was a nice guy with tired eyes who had understandable suspicions about my impartiality as a witness, given my close friendship with the driver. He seemed sympathetic, while providing the obligatory reminders of my legal responsibilities.

"Remember," he said, "you can't get in trouble for telling the truth. But you can get in a lot of trouble for lying."

What happened? I knew, but I didn't really have a clue.

We were driving along the New England Highway towards Toowoomba. I wasn't paying much attention and then I looked up and thought we were heading into a yard or something and then we went through the trees and got hit on the other side.

Dom was sober. Prior to losing control he was driving normally. It didn't seem like he was going fast. It happened suddenly. As far as I'm aware everyone was behaving normally in the car.

After we got hit I remember bouncing up and looking around. I saw some people come over. I looked in the back and saw all the boys. I remember seeing blood and it looked like everyone was sleeping. Some of them made funny sounds like they were snoring.

Someone yelled turn the car off. I reached over for the keys but couldn't find them. I remember someone pulled me through the driver's side window.

I got out of the car but I couldn't really remember what happened. I sat down for a while somewhere. I remember I called my sister and she came to get me.

On May 18, 2009, I attended the Toowoomba Police Station. I have no further information in relation to this matter.

At the end of the interview, I signed five sheets of paper declaring that I wasn't lying. A weight lifted off my shoulders. I looked at the cop optimistically, as though he might announce Dom's exoneration. We could piece our shattered lives together with privacy.

"I'll ring you when we need you to come back," he said.

"What for?"

"We've only just started sifting through the evidence. More will come to light. So we'll need to do some more interviews."

I asked the officer how long the legal process might take, thinking in months, worried that a court case might interrupt the bliss of graduation and Schoolies Week.

"Just the investigation?" he asked.

"And then if it goes to court."

"Criminal cases can take years."

The car crash wasn't over. It was just getting started.

NICK WAS OFFICIALLY A MIRACLE. Doctors had at first predicted that he would need twenty-four-hour care for the rest of his life. Yet three weeks after the car crash, he'd been transferred from the Gold Coast to the brain injury rehabilitation unit at Toowoomba Hospital. Now neurologists believed he'd make a full recovery. I staged sleepovers on the La-Z-Boy beside his bed. We watched slapstick comedies.

Nick was exhausted from learning how to walk and talk again, but he saw it as a fair sacrifice for friendship. "I'm glad this happened to me," he said, "and not you."

"What's that supposed to mean?" I asked.

"I'm used to getting knocked out. And breaking shit. I don't think you would've woken up. If you were in the trunk."

"Is this your heroic way of calling me a *pussy*?"

"Nah. But yeah. You're a bit of a pussy."

"Thanks. You took a coma for the team."

A snicker knocked the wind from his lungs. "Bones heal, bro," he said.

Nick's rapid improvement was bittersweet. I envisioned Tim following suit, but day after day he stayed deeply asleep in the state capital. My best mate had been transferred from ICU to the high dependence unit, but was stuck at five on the Glasgow Coma Scale.

I took a Friday off from school to pay him a visit.

"Timmy," said Linda. "Lech is here to see you."

I watched Tim's eyelids for a flutter, but they stayed stubbornly shut. A hose in his windpipe provided oxygen. Tubes through the nostrils filled his stomach with food.

"I'll leave you guys to have a chat. Tell him to wake up, hey?"

I sat silently beside Tim, suffocated by the strange and dangerous weight of all the painful phrases that I was aching and incapable of saying to him.

Wake up. My life is over without you.

"Pray for him," said Linda. "We need a miracle, Lech."

Tim believed in God. He was morally opposed to smoking. I saw human beings as intelligent chimpanzees. Our friendship was like a parable: the optimistic bricklayer and the pessimistic poet.

This was always the biggest schism between us. Optimism never made any sense to me.

• • • •

ON THE PENULTIMATE DAY of autumn, the upper crust of an extinct volcano came together for a famous game of rugby union. *Grammar vs. Downlands.* It was an annual tradition for rival private-school alumni to dress primly and watch blood-thirsty teenage boys ruck and scrum each other into surrender, before burying the hatchet by getting hammered together at the Spotted Cow Hotel.

The paper declared the glitz and glamour must go on in the wake of a tragedy that made old passions seem irrational. "We need to approach it as another game of rugby," said Grammar's head prefect and rugby union captain. "It has to be First XV on First XV."

On the morning of the game, I went clothes shopping with my father. Normally he'd just give me fifty dollars from the till, but recent events had made him feel guilty about skipping out. So we endured some excruciating male bonding at a department store called Hannas. I tried on Ralph Lauren polos with cream chinos.

"Are you sure that pony on the shirt is big enough?" he blurted. "The conservative recruiters won't be able to see ya."

The parents of my new friends were right-wing farmers and white-collar professionals. One of them was the grandson of the agricultural minister in a right-wing government. Not only was I partying with the enemy, now I wanted to dress like them too.

Dad was about to play lawn bowls. His thick sideburns matched his shirt, trousers, and shoes in colour. He belonged to a cabal of left-wing drinkers at a clubhouse filled with right-wing retirees.

"You look like a sunburnt Colonel Sanders," I said.

My father coughed with mock outrage, but the banter broke the ice between us. He said, "Get whatever you want," before noticing me eyeing a pair of four-hundred-dollar R.M.Williams boots. "You're pulling my dick, aren't ya? Buckley's chance my son will be seen dead in a pair of those fuckin' things."

I went home to get showered and dressed. The PR system at the race club was publicising winners to the surrounding houses as I pulled up. Country music blared from the radio in the kitchen. My mother was chain-smoking menthol cigarettes beside the Jacuzzi on the back patio of our souring Australian dream.

Mum came inside and cracked open a can of rum and cola with a dessert spoon, due to her arthritis, while inspecting the designer outfit paid for by her rival.

"You look *beautiful*," she said, incapable of negative feedback. "Did your tight-arse father pay for that? Good one."

I drove away without a goodbye kiss. Sheets of corrugated steel spread like melanomas across a sunburnt horizon, answering the cancer of drought with the radiation of real estate. In the steep east, Queens Park remained green. Lavish gardens shielded the courtyards where mothers drank shiraz instead of rum, different stiffeners for matching Lexapro prescriptions.

At Grammar, I approached a festival of prosperity with anthropological fascination. Gothic buildings soared above hills filled with boys chanting vaguely pagan slogans. They wore grey Akubra hats and blue blazers with yellow pin-stripes. Botox saved grinning mothers the inevitable wrinkles of parenthood. Fathers wore R.M.Williams boots and brave expressions on their faces.

"WHO'S GOT THE CUP?" barked the heirs to vast agricultural empires. "*WHO'S GOT THE CUP?*"

The question was rhetorical. Grammar had won four of the last five cups, including a twenty-one-point thrashing the previous year.

Downlands supporters congregated opposite, blazers darker but blood a lighter shade of blue. Their privilege was seen as kitsch due to the glitch of Catholicism and the fact they never gained full admission to the GPS, a clique of elite rugby union schools. This was a vital source of self-esteem for Grammar, who in turn were seen as hillbillies by the Brisbane GPS schools, who were viewed as hicks by the truly rich in Sydney and Melbourne. This was the harsh secret of the Australian dream: no matter how high you flew, there was always some other bastard above you.

"Fire up, Downlands, fire up!" the underdogs chanted.

I stood with Dom and Nick, as a tight-knit trio of survivors made their first public appearance together. Dom still had his collarbone in a sling. Nick was in a wheelchair, gruesome scars splayed across a pale forehead.

Dom grinned at Nick with thinly veiled guilt. "How ya feeling?" he asked.

"I wish I was playing," Nick said.

The most unsettling thing for Nick to witness wasn't the match, but how seamlessly I'd replaced him. "Everyone keeps sucking your dick," Nick muttered, and I laughed, but he wasn't hallucinating. I was *cool*, that elusive quality usually monopolised by the rich, beautiful, or athletically exceptional. Ever since the car crash, people wanted to meet me.

There was a minute's silence for Will, Hamish, and Henry. Downlands supporters gaped into blank space, yearning for an alternative present. Athletes on high-protein diets wore skintight jerseys and black armbands for the dead.

"Get me a jersey," the missing outside centre whispered.

Nick was the one player who inspired blind faith in teammates and fear in rivals. The truest way he knew to honour the memory of the departed was to see Grammar annihilated. But without him, Downlands didn't stand a chance.

The first half was a bloodbath. Fumbles and forward passes reigned supreme. Panicked teenagers couldn't live up to the weight of expectation from nostalgic fathers, or prospective girlfriends with fussy mothers. Along the packed sidelines, anticipation for a nail-biter dissipated. Grammar ran out to a 22–3 lead.

Nick suffered from FOMO. As he watched Downlands lose, all his friends discussed plans to get to the afterparty.

"I wish I was coming out," he mumbled at half-time.

"It won't be *that* great," I said.

"Piss off, Lech. It's gonna be hectic."

"Nah, it'll probably get shut down by ten."

"If it's gonna be so shit, come to the hospital."

I tried to think of a way to change the subject.

"That's what I thought," he said.

In the second half, Downlands added respectability with a belated try, but the game was over. Grammar won 22–10. Blue-and-yellow blazers flapped across the oval. The rival captains lifted the cup jointly towards the heavens.

The afterparty was at Vincent's mansion. I drove there with Dom. We had become inseparable on weekends. The two survivors who escaped without brain damage could trust each other not to highlight that luck, or to judge the numbness underpinning our continuing social activities and alcohol consumption.

"What did you think of the game?" he asked.

"Boring as batshit," I said. "But don't tell anyone I said that."

At Vincent's, we were welcomed by the same faces from the vigils and wakes, except now they were smiling. The partygoers had gathered on a timber balcony above the swimming pool. Girls kissed my cheek. Guys competed to give me a beer.

Frida hugged me. We walked along the pristine lawn overlooking the Great Dividing Range.

"How are you holding up?" she asked. "And don't give me that cliché bullshit about *hanging in there.*"

"I don't really know yet," I said, caught off guard.

"You don't have to talk about it."

It was rare for someone to ask about my mental wellbeing with aspirations to a complicated answer.

"It's not that hard to talk about. It's sort of too easy to say something that doesn't mean anything."

"But as long as you can say *that,*" said Frida.

"What do you mean?"

"Like, just admit the emptiness of it all."

In the background, the Lockyer Valley was a mosaic of lime and beige acres spreading hazily to the horizon. The distant outer limits of Brisbane faded away until they blurred with the sky.

"I don't know if the words exist to admit the emptiness," I said.

"That's perfect! You aren't supposed to have the right words."

We went back upstairs. The farms turned black. Cars on the highway looked like slow shooting stars.

On Millionaires' Row, minors smoked cigarettes and swallowed Jägerbombs to the same soundtrack as the summer. Alcohol quarantined me from the hospital visits.

This is how grim spirits become kindred.

This is how numbness becomes a ritual.

After midnight, most of the party went home and Vincent raided the wine cellar. We drank merlots and cabernet sauvignons in red plastic cups left over from games of beer pong. Mineral water and Doritos sobered up those of us sleeping over.

"It feels wrong to fall asleep," sighed Frida.

In the cinema, Vincent put on *Anchorman.* A dozen bodies dropped across couches and spare mattresses.

"I'm Ron Burgundy," muttered a guy on the brink of sleep.

It was the first film Tim and I saw together at the movies. We'd recite the quotes so often they became involuntary.

Frida's lips found mine in the murk.

"Who even are you?" she murmured.

I was a well-spoken redneck from a broken home.

The carefree behaviour of the day just gone made me ashamed to still be breathing. I thought about where I was forty-eight hours earlier: visiting Tim.

Frida curved assertively against me, but I couldn't manage anything sensual. She sighed and fell asleep. Her limbs twitched every now and then, as though they were being zapped with a cattle prod. I shut my eyes so that I didn't feel like a creep.

When I opened them again, sunlight flooded through the shutters, uncovering a roomful of spooning teenagers. Frida and I kissed one more time just for existing.

• • • •

AUTUMN PASSED ITS EXPIRY DATE. Red leaves ringed the trees like campfires. Subscribers fetched papers from thawing lawns. Our faces were replaced on the front pages.

Death was everywhere that winter, but the main danger was swine flu. Mexican pigs had spread the virus to farmers before it mutated and became an international smash hit.

Journalists reported feverishly on the disproven hoaxes that their coverage promoted. "Swine flu has *not* spread to Toowoomba," wrote a journalist. "But the city is in the grip of a rumour pandemic."

Frida and I had agreed to see a movie before exams, but one of my classmates tested positive. St. Mary's students went into a two-week quarantine. The 99.99 per cent of pupils without swine flu fist-pumped and high-fived the delayed exams.

I guess we'll have to delay that date, Frida texted.

We can die of swine flu together, I said. *It'll be a Shakespearean tragedy for Generation Y*

I want a doctor's certificate saying you are swine-free

For a fortnight, I watched footage of vaccines getting stockpiled and farm animals being herded into sacrificial abattoirs. The death toll for pig influenza stayed in the single digits, making it less deadly than the common type.

Massive overreaction, I said. *It's just the flu. Not syphilis you should get tested for that too*

On the first Saturday night of the winter holidays, I borrowed my father's black Ford Falcon XR6—which looked vaguely like a Mercedes-Benz—to take Frida on a belated first date. At the Drayton Tavern, I waited for my father to finish pouring schooners.

"You got a missus?" he asked.

"Nah," I said. "Not yet."

"Why don't you bring her out here for a feed?"

The main attraction on the menu was the Drayton Dream, a seventeen-ounce rump steak covered with butter, garlic, mushrooms, and mozzarella, served with beer-battered chips and vegetables.

"She's vegetarian," I said.

"Get her the garlic bread, big fella!"

Greyhound racing was interrupted by breaking news about Michael Jackson suffering a fatal overdose.

"Someone finally shut that poofter up," shouted a plumber. "Ya hear about his toaster?" asked a plasterer. "The bread goes in brown. And comes out white!"

Customers in his vicinity laughed hysterically, lips dry from beef jerky and fingertips oily from boiled peanuts. It was my job to rinse their spew from the piss troughs on Saturday and Sunday mornings, before doing a split shift in the kitchen.

My father's pride and joy was a thick wad of fifty-dollar notes folded in his wallet. He slipped me one. "Take her somewhere nice. And remember to tarp up!"

"You're a grub," I said, blushing.

Fog wafted democratically between the trough of Drayton and the peak of Rangeville. Frida's home was an architect's impression of a French château. The electric security gates were open. I knocked on a tall front door. Frida wore a black cashmere sweater tucked into jeans, bare feet displaying white toenails.

"I'm not ready," she said. "Michael Jackson is dead!"

Frida sat down on the couch to put on a pair of sneakers. The living room brimmed with minimalist design. I studied pictures of Frida's photogenic parents stuck to the fridge.

"Do your parents go out much?" I asked.

"Yeah. They have a busier social life than me."

Her gaze was still glued to the TV. The media were staging a seventy-two-hour celebration of a man they'd spent a decade accusing of pedophilia.

I was hurt by Frida's lack of attention after waiting so impatiently to regain it. "It's nice to see you again too," I said.

Frida lifted a finger to her lips. The reporter buzzed with the possibility of murder, before the coverage cut to an ad for life insurance. "I'm grieving!" she said.

The conspiracy theories continued on a different channel. Frida sensed my contempt. She launched an impassioned defence of MJ's artistic legacy. "He changed the way singers sound and look," she said.

"Well, I've never understood why someone that rich would want to change the way they look."

"Of course not. You're white."

Frida told me about the nasty comments before and after September 11, and how an Anglo mother caught a hyphenated daughter scrubbing at her limbs with exfoliating gloves.

Frida, she asked. *What are you doing?*
I'm trying to wash the brown off.
"You don't need to be a freak to wish you were white," said Frida.
"You're right," I said. "I'm an idiot."
A tanned hand with long fingers touched my arm. "Sorry for the lecture!" she said. "Great start to the date."
We drove to the city centre. I parked on Margaret Street, named after the Queen's self-destructive younger sister. The Strand Theatre was maligned for rigid armrests that prevented teenagers from reaching second base.
I bought two tickets to *Disgrace,* an adaptation of the J.M. Coetzee novel—trying to prove that I was cultivated enough for Frida to date me—plus an extra-large popcorn and two frozen Cokes.
"Hey, big spender," said Frida. "Thanks."
"It's my pleasure."
"The pleasure is all mine."
I was soon quite certain that I wouldn't be on the receiving end of any pleasure from Frida, that night or ever again. "A movie about rape on our first date," she whispered. "Such a sweet guy."
"Coetzee won the Nobel Prize!"
"That's not going to get you laid."
Afterwards, we stopped at McDonald's to buy McFlurrys. Then we drove to Picnic Point, where a floodlit flag hung limply over a kingdom of tennis courts, swimming pools, and teenagers receiving patriotic BJS.
Frida squinted at the static flag through the misted windshield. "I *love* a sunburnt country!" she said.
I leaned over to kiss her, our lips still salty from popcorn and tongues sweetened by ice cream. But the romantic atmosphere was eroded by a Subaru WRX ripping a burnout.
"Let's go home," said Frida. "Before my parents get back."

We returned to the eastern hinterland. Frida led me to her bedroom by the hand. Vinyl albums were stacked against a record player, Lauryn Hill and 2 Pac adjacent to Patti Smith and Bach. Frida put on *Graduation* by Kanye West and lowered the volume.

"What do you want to do?" she asked.

"I dunno," I said. "Listen to music?"

Frida peeled my polo shirt off and pushed me against the linen sheets. Now her T-shirt and jeans were off, revealing a cream bra, and then no briefs. I went down on Frida, who was proudly unshaven. This was more exhilarating than sex, because I got the endorsement of her desire without the performance anxiety.

"Do you have a condom?" she asked.

Her confidence astonished me. I'd assumed that Frida was a virgin. She'd assumed that I wasn't. We were both wrong. I'd never been undressed in front of someone while sober.

"No," I said. "I didn't think..."

Frida pulled one from a drawer. She turned the lights off before removing my chinos and jocks and guiding me inside. I thrusted, too quickly, for a few minutes. Frida climbed on top.

"Slow down," she whispered.

Frida directed me at different angles and speeds to those in the pornos I'd grown up studying. But I was too distracted to climax, a Romeo who lived and fornicated in the third person.

Afterwards, we lay together touching and kissing, grinning like we'd just invented sex.

"I hope you don't think that I'm clingy," said Frida, with uncharacteristic sincerity. "But I love you, Lech Blaine."

"I love you too," I said, slightly irritated that Frida put into words what I was saving until it was a slam-dunk.

"Great," said Frida. "I'm officially dating a St. Mary's boy. My mother will be mortified! Which reminds me: you need to go."

Her parents weren't due home for another hour, but I was happy to leave, believing I'd bridged the distance between a solicitor's daughter and a bartender's son.

I had one more life-or-death question to ask before departing. "So I was w-w-wondering..." I stuttered.

"Yes," said Frida.

"And you can definitely say no."

"Are you proposing to me?"

"Whether you wanted to come to my formal."

"What took you so long to ask?"

On the way home, the defoggers whispered against the windshield. "Billie Jean" played from the MJ vigil on the radio. I was alone but no longer lonely.

As my tires hit the driveway, I got a text from Frida.

Damnit, Lech Blaine. You tricked me!

How do you mean?

I wasn't supposed to fall in love before exams

My mother was snoring like a chainsaw on the couch in the lounge room. The coffee table was cluttered with empty rum cans.

"Tonight: the world is crying tears for Michael Jackson," said a reporter. "After the ad break, we count down the ten most tragic celebrity deaths of all time."

I turned it off and kissed my mother on the cheek.

Nothing could encroach on my romantic momentum.

Lucky I'm such a catch, I wrote to Frida.

I do feel lucky, she said.

Likewise. You make life happen more to me

that's a nice thing to say. Talk to you tomorrow xxx

In my bedroom, before sleep, I scrolled through Frida's Facebook profile to keep at a safe distance all the other things I couldn't bring myself to think about.

Guilty
Parties

AND THEN THE SEASONS CHANGED. Everyone forgot about swine flu and Michael Jackson. Toowoomba homeowners began their preoccupation with botany, competing for the attention of a fickle audience with rationed H_2O. The Garden City was famous for two things: voting no to recycled water, and wasting millions of kilotons of the stuff on the annual Carnival of Flowers.

"Spring is sprung!" my mother sang.

That day, at exactly the same time statewide, Grade Twelvers would begin forty-eight hours of final exams.

Dom texted in the morning. *Did you see the front page???* he asked.

A newspaper was on the kitchen table. The headshots of Henry, Will, and Hamish grinned above the headline.

Chilling new evidence on Downlands tragedy: POLICE SEIZE VIDEO FROM DEAD BOY'S FAMILY

Beneath each half-Windsor knot was the word DEAD.

Page 3 featured a photo of the wreck above a portrait of the driver, who wore a smile.

Police have seized a chilling video depicting the final seconds before Downlands College student Dom Hodal lost control of his car, leaving three of his best friends dead. It is believed Henry, who was sitting in the back of the 1989 Ford Fairlane, recorded video footage which cut out just seconds before the fatal head-on crash at Highfields.

According to unnamed sources, police executed a search warrant on Henry's family home, confiscating his mobile. They sent the SIM card to the forensic examination unit in Brisbane.

On the opposite page, three high achievers from Grammar held pens above textbooks, cramming for exams, forming a juxtaposition of youthful innocence and annihilation.

"It is really important we feel well prepared," said the prefect, "but we have a lot of other work to do."

Inside the St. Mary's hall, everyone was gripped by the existence of the video. It was the Zapruder film of a municipal tragedy. Rumours circulated that the footage confirmed all of the most far-fetched innuendo. The biggest crackpots claimed to have seen a leaked copy.

I was saved from distraction by a caveman response to the late-capitalist struggle for social mobility. I wanted to get into the same sandstone campus as Frida: the University of Queensland.

"You may begin the test," said a teacher. "Good luck!"

There was a reflection task and a short-response task. The topic of the reflection task was "time." I was only seventeen, but I had time enough for seven people.

The next day brought two multiple-choice exams. I remained in a state of flow, focused only on the questions and the answers.

On Wednesday afternoon, as my classmates skylarked in the car park, I drove to the police station to give another statement about an event that I was expected to remember and then forget, to forget and then remember again. A detective had called the day before. It was to be my sixth interrogation.

The law-and-order precinct sat opposite Queens Park, the botanical heart of the Garden City. The station was bigger and shinier than the courthouse. We sat in a larger interview room than normal. A laptop was plugged into an LCD television. The screen showed the opening still of the seized footage. The contrast had been adjusted, clarifying the shadows into recognisable faces.

The cop said, "Are you ready to roll?"

"Yeah, mate. I'm sweet."

"Just let me know if it gets too much."

Henry panned around the moving vehicle. We were singing "Wonderwall." From the trunk, Nick stuck his hand through a speaker hole, waving the red tip of a cigarette.

The karaoke petered out. Henry aimed the lens towards the front, where the mood was more subdued. I was looking at my iPhone. The speedometer showed that Dom was driving a few klicks under the speed limit.

The video blacked out abruptly. Within the next fifteen seconds, our gold Ford Fairlane had careered across the median strip and collided with the blue Holden Viva.

"It makes you wonder," said the police officer, "what made him stop filming. Like he knew something was about to happen."

I disagreed with the cop. Life's biggest moments generally occur when we aren't trying to capture them. If something dramatic were about to happen, Henry would've kept the camera going. He filmed what seemed like the most memorable sequence of the evening.

The detective replayed the footage three more times, frustrated by a gun that wouldn't smoke. Each rewind made me feel more dead inside. The video was so close to solving the mystery that marked my survival with an asterisk, but instead it muddied the waters: how does life transit so quickly from innocence to obliteration?

• • • •

FRIDA AND I HAD SLEPT TOGETHER half a dozen more times. Yet as she fretted about exams and final piano recitals, the chemistry between us hit the skids. I blamed her lack of interest on my continuing inability to orgasm.

sorry for being such a flake, Frida wrote after another last-minute cancellation. *don't take it personally.*

The fickleness of her attention made me lovesick.

I won't, I wrote. *I know you're under the pump.*

The truth was that my entire nervous system had caught fire, incandescent with a fear of abandonment. This made me morose whenever Frida called, and even more physically distant when we saw each other.

"You need to relax," she said, after I accepted a hand job with the enthusiasm of a tetanus shot.

Then Frida was prohibited from driving with me late at night. Her parents—whom I still hadn't met—introduced a 9:00 PM road curfew until graduation.

why? I asked. *what did you do?*

I didn't do anything, she wrote. *my parents realised that their daughter's new chauffeur has a few black marks against his name*

because I was in the crash???

it's a combination of factors

what are the other factors?

A: you don't go to Grammar, and B: a Real Housewife of Rangeville told my mother that you smoke crack and belong to a gang of drag racers

Now, during any delay in communication, I visualised the six-pack of the camera-friendly mannequin from Grammar that Frida's mother wanted to replace me with.

what do they think I'm going to do with you? I asked. *drive us off the quarry? Romeo and Juliet meets Rebel Without a Cause?*

they just don't want me to get pregnant before university. and you don't strike them as a celibate

For a week after the exams, the longest I slept was three hours. On Friday morning, I rose and resisted having a cigarette before showering and swapping cars with Dad.

"Just don't be too smart by half," he warned. "This girl will know who you are soon enough. And no one likes a pretender."

"Right. That's why your love life is booming."

"How about ya fill the tank for once?"

Fuck you, cunt, I thought. Then: *I'm the cunt.*

That afternoon, I idled behind European SUVs while trying to spot Frida at her private school. The rear windshields of four-wheel drives were plastered with sports emblems featuring Roman numerals.

Frida dumped her bag on the back seat and climbed in the front. She stank of stale sweat and fresh deodorant. A baggy dress veiled any hint of skin above the knee. Face makeup free, black hair in a ponytail. Her laughter was a password from the past to the present.

"Your parents have done me a favour," I said. "That's hot."

"Thanks, babe," she said. "But am I *hawt*, or just *hot?*"

"My sincere apologies. H-A-W-T, definitely."

We drove to Grand Central Shopping Centre. Inside the cinema, the scent of popcorn evoked a generalised memory of the Thursday nights I spent there hanging out with Tim.

"Are you okay?" asked Frida.

"Yeah," I said. "Why's that?"

"You seem a bit far away today."

Frida mistook my silence for indignation that she had chosen to see *Harry Potter and the Half-Blood Prince*. We'd recently debated the literary merits of J.K. Rowling.

"How have you never *seen* a Harry Potter film?" she asked in the queue. "Like, I can understand not reading the books. But not seeing the movies? That's not even remotely cool. It's just weird."

"I had an old-fashioned childhood. No PlayStations or Xboxes. And none of this fantasy bullshit."

"What did you do for *fun* in primary school? Watch the football and horseracing? Play the slot machines?"

"No!" I snapped, recalling my father's warning.

"Excuse me for picking what *I* wanted to see. After you took me to a rape movie. You were lucky to get a second date."

I wanted to flee from the disagreement.

But during the movie, Frida was gripped by a religious experience. A bookworm virgin underwent puberty and confronted first love while battling against a terrorist cell of genocidal wizards and witches called the Death Eaters, who kept hijacking his attempts to be a normal teenager.

Afterwards, Frida linked arms with me like nothing had happened. We streamed out with kids dressed as wizards.

"So, Hemingway," she said, "what's your verdict?"

"That was pretty good," I said.

"Pretty relatable for a bunch of wizards, huh?"

We had roughly two hours to kill before Frida's curfew. Unlike me, she had given some thought to the window of opportunity for sex. "How about we go to your place?"

"Probably not."

"Why?"

I realised with horror there was absolutely no logical reason why I couldn't take Frida home. I'd been banking on an unspoken assumption that she suffered from an allergic reaction to the western suburbs.

"It'll take ages," I said. "We won't make curfew."

"Our houses are fifteen minutes apart."

"I haven't cleaned my room."

"Seriously, Lech. Start the car. We're going there."

We drove past St. Mary's, the garage, and the unlit race-course. "This is nice," said Frida, and a rational part of me knew that she was right. Glenvale was a perfectly liveable aspirational suburb. But I'd become so paranoid about class that I couldn't unsee the lack of Range Rovers in the driveways.

The door to the house was open, but I nudged Frida towards the granny flat.

"Aren't we going to say hi to your parents?" she asked.

"They'll be asleep," I said.

"It's pretty much dinnertime," she said.

"They're early risers."

"Let's at least check."

I was overcome with frustration. It had been a sleepless week and a draining date and now there was this hunt for the existence of my separated parents.

"Fuck me, Frida. Mind your own business."

"*Okay*," she whispered.

In the musty granny flat, my queen mattress was covered in unfinished novels. The fraying carpet was littered with dirty clothes and empty packets of cigarettes. I stacked the books on a bedside table and rushed to dispose of the laundry.

"I didn't realise you smoked so much," said Frida.

"I'm quitting," I said. "I just haven't tidied up in ages."

I sat on the edge of the bed. My plastic CD player was designed to look like a gramophone. Frida selected The National's *Boxer*. The sparring pianos of "Fake Empire" oozed into my inelegant suburban bedroom.

"I can play this," she said.

Frida turned the light off. She unzipped her dress and slipped it to the floor, revealing grey briefs and a black sports bra. Then she unknotted the tie from my collar.

"Am I leading you into temptation?" she asked.

"Absolutely."

For a while, I did a credible job convincing Frida I was in the same frame of mind. We played games of cat-and-mouse with lips and fingers. I had a condom proximate. On a purely acrobatic level, the sex seemed better than usual. But I felt nothing except a crushing sense of frustration.

Frida broke her own rule against giving blow jobs. Ten minutes felt like three hours. Eventually, I rolled over and sat naked on the edge of the bed. It was as if my brain and body had been drained of the capacity for pleasure, and instead saturated with shame.

"What's wrong?" asked Frida.

"Nothing," I said.

"I just want you to feel good."

"It doesn't. Tonight. For some reason."

We were both humiliated.

"Why would you let me do that, then?" she asked.

I couldn't answer the question honestly without admitting to unfixable glitches. Cicadas hummed beneath the windowsill.

"We better go," said Frida. "It's getting late."

We headed for Frida's place via the hospital that contained death and the cathedral that failed to explain it.

"Can you stop at Picnic Point?" she said. "We need to talk."

"What about?" I asked.

Frida chewed her lip nervously, as if it was a high-school debate and she was worried about delivering the argument within the time limit. "Us," she said.

I parked between the flagpole and the water tower. The silhouette of Table Top Mountain soared across the unlit valley.

Frida burst into tears. She delivered the predictable breakup script for a relationship that hadn't existed long enough to be made Facebook official.

"I can't keep seeing you," she said. "It's too much pressure."

"You're breaking up with me," I said.

"Yeah."

Clearly, Frida couldn't keep seeing *me*.

"But you were in love with me," I said.

"I know."

"So now you don't love me?"

"I don't know! Not enough. Not right now."

The red fog light above the blue flag looked less like a beacon of possibility and more like a traffic light. *You silly bastard*, I thought, in my father's voice. I was a latter-day Jay Gatsby, that famous fraud, craving the saving grace of a giddy rich kid from the eastern suburbs.

Frida seemed relieved to get the truth off her chest, but slightly offended by my lack of visible distress.

"Are you upset?" she asked.

"Not really. I saw the writing on the wall."

"It's terrifying. You notice everything."

"Thanks."

Frida held my hand tenderly. "I still *really* want to come to your formal."

"Right."

"That's if you want me to."

"Sure. It'll be fun."

Now she looked at the time, adding insult to injury. It was quarter past nine.

Outside the house, Frida kissed me weakly on the cheek. "I'm here if you need me," she said. "Remember that."

"No worries," I mumbled.

I parked outside for five minutes, stalled in a loading zone of loneliness, until the shape of Frida's mother appeared through the screen door. I started the car and drove home.

In our lounge room, my mother sat on the La-Z-Boy reading a book. "Hey, baby," she said, noticeably sober, which meant that she would have been highly capable of charming my ex-girlfriend.

"Hey, Mum," I said.

I lay down on the worn-out couch.

"How has your week been?" she asked.

"I've had better," I said.

"It's like that sometimes."

She slapped her book onto the stack next to the couch. Mazda sneezed outside cobwebbed sliding doors, collar rattling as he scratched at fleas.

"Having me as a mother might not seem like winning the lotto," she said. "But I won the jackpot with you. Twice."

"What was the first time?"

"Your birth! It was the happiest day of my life."

I was suffocated by guilt for concealing her earlier.

"I love you, Lech," she said. "I wouldn't trade you for all the diamonds in a mine, or all the money in a mint."

I stayed on the couch and wept, overcome with the drug of too much love at once after so many numb years of hunting around for something to feel that good.

• • • •

ON THE THIRD SATURDAY of September, tourists ascended the Great Dividing Range for the Carnival of Flowers, eating corn dogs while smiling absently at mobile flowerbeds. In the holidays, as jacarandas spewed purple confetti onto the footpaths, a plume larger than Germany travelled rapidly towards Queensland. Near-hurricane-level winds sucked up dust from the South Australian desert, bushfire smoke from Victoria, and red dirt from farms in New South Wales.

The Garden City was hit by a crimson mist, causing drivers to collide. Drugstores were stripped of asthma puffers, while agile hypochondriacs recycled masks purchased for the aborted swine-flu epidemic.

"Are the dust storms radioactive?" wondered news.com.au.

I stayed inside listening to Sufjan Stevens while watching TV footage of a disaster unfolding behind the blinds. The evaporation of the dust made no difference. I felt free and defeated, pretending the war was over, like a soldier decompressing before redeployment.

Vincent—who was officially dating Frida's friend Anna—knew all about the breakup. In an effort to improve my mood, he proposed starting a band. During winter, I had introduced him to Pavement and the Silver Jews. Now he was equally obsessed with them.

Vincent played guitar. I wrote poetry. I named the band Negative Gearing as an ironic nod to the tax loophole that turned my father into a real estate investor. Vincent started scouting a bassist and drummer.

"We've got enough songs for an EP," he said.

"Don't get ahead of yourself," I said, but it was exhilarating to show the sensitive side of my soul to someone without editing the melancholia.

Nick was offended by how much time I was spending with Vincent. After a miraculous recovery, he had gone back to school, and was drinking with more abandon than before, because in the short term he didn't have a sports career.

"What are you two pussies doing?" he asked.

"None of your business," I said.

Our relationship had always functioned on the basis that Nick was the alpha athlete, and me his beta sidekick. Now I got invited to parties without him, because people were uncomfortable about Nick drinking again. His visible scars elicited awkward pauses.

"You're a dog," he said.

On a Saturday night, I skipped pre-drinks at Nick's place for a rival gathering in East Toowoomba. Eight passengers packed into a Maxi Taxi. All the parties that spring were out past the crash site in Highfields. The minibus rattled to the destination. Slammed doors and revving engines merged with the DOOF-DOOF-DOOF pulsating from the dance tent, which loomed like a lighthouse at the heart of a dark farm.

I stormed into the party costumed as a normal teenager without gloom in my heart or doom in my dreams. Silver bags of wine shone from the clothesline.

There is no aphrodisiac like tragedy. Two hundred teenagers danced and tested the strength of attractions as faces flickered in strobe lights. We choked on artificial smoke. Skin touched skin. Eyes were lit up by the flames of raging bonfires, limbs shivering and tongues substituting spit.

Around the bonfire, someone poured a medley of whatever drinks were at hand—beer, bourbon, fruit-flavoured vodka—into one of his R.M.Williams boots. Someone else handed me a Gatorade bong, which I ripped before chugging the entire contents of the shoey.

"Here's to Blainey," sang the party, "he's true blue, he's a pisspot through and through, he's a bastard, so they say. He was meant to go to heaven, but he went the other way. So, SCULL! SCULL! SCULL!"

I planted the boot upside down on my head and blew the residue from the bong hit towards the starlit sky.

"What do we think of Blainey? He's all right!"

This was the bleak paradox of fame: my popularity and loneliness reached a peak at the same moment.

The mood of the party edged towards aggressive. A boarder from Downlands headbutted a St. Mary's boy before peppering him with uppercuts. I stood on the Downlands side during the brawl.

Police showed up like morticians at a swingers' party. Sirens spun across the tree trunks. The DJ switched the music off. Sergeants charged through paddocks and aimed flashlights at underage teens approaching third base.

"Show's over, folks!" yelled a cop. "Time to go home."

Two hundred drunk teenagers flooded towards the New England Highway. An empty bottle shattered against the black-top, while a second fight threatened to erupt.

My sister was already on her way to pick me up. I divvied up the three remaining seats. Nick recognised the getaway vehicle and intercepted me about to leave.

"Where are you going?" he asked.

"Home," I said.

"Sweet. I'll come with you."

"Sorry, mate. We've got a full car."

On the highway liable for the scar on his skull, Nick glared at a back seat packed to capacity without him.

"You've changed, Lech," he said.

"Since when?" I said, smirking to cover the hurt.

"Since the crash. You think you're better than me."

He was right: I had changed. I was more popular and increasingly arrogant, a smokescreen for my sorrow.

"Fuck off, Nick," I said. "Find your own lift."

In two months, I was relocating to Brisbane for university. Nick was an anchor to a tragic chapter of my uncouth youth that I needed to leave behind. He wasn't blameless in the end of our friendship, but I let him slip away without a whimper.

Going home, the roadside shrine flickered through a slit in the median strip, but my gaze didn't stray.

Rebel With a Stress Disorder

THROUGHOUT A DROUGHT-STRICKEN SPRING, as dams nudged towards empty, Tim remained in the hospital. His parents had quit their jobs and moved to Brisbane. For months, medical experts worked tirelessly to reanimate the neural pathways among his brain cells. Finally, Tim's eyelids opened.

When I visited, the patient was capable of answering *yes* to questions by blinking. His mother asked, "Do you remember Lech?" and Tim blinked.

Other visitors celebrated. I feigned elation, but eye contact caused an eruption of suffering. Tim could see the difference between us. The breakthrough ruined my delusion that once a patient wakes up from a coma, they go straight back to normal. *This* was the new normal: painstaking improvements to a permanent brain injury.

"I'm not going to piss in your pocket and tell you it's raining," said Dad. "There aren't going to be any miracles."

The St. Mary's Old Boys started a charity drive to raise money for Tim's rehabilitation. On Saturday afternoons, I sold raffle tickets at the tavern, hawking sports memorabilia in return for small amounts of tax-deductible compassion.

"How's Tom doin'?" asked a Keno player.

"Tim," I said.

"I meant Tim! How is the bloke?"

A silence was punctured by jingles from one of the slot ·
machines.

"He's hanging in there," I said.

"It ain't over till the fat lady sings. Remember that."

The fundraiser was held on a mild Saturday night. In Centenary Court, a string section serenaded dusk-lit tables. For once, there were no apples or muesli bars flying from one end of the courtyard to the other. Instead, students in navy blazers plied stylish patrons with premium beers and flutes of champagne.

For the past three years, Tim and I had worked as waiters for the Old Boys Association, serving drinks and rib fillets at fundraisers just like this one.

I went to the dinner with Dom and Nick. At a slight distance from the mingling adults, we sat on the same bench where I had met Nick as a ten-year-old, but the location didn't rekindle the friendship between us.

I filed inside for dinner with a fake smile and sat at a table near the heart of the packed hall. Onlookers regarded me with menacing levels of sympathy.

Someone said, "Just imagine if Tim could be here to see this!"

Photos of Tim were projected onto the screen at the front of a hall where the two of us had whispered to each other during assemblies for five years.

Adults buttered bread rolls and prepared bids for rare collector items, hissing small talk to distract each other from the missing dinner guest. It seemed insane that all of these well-meaning people could keep their shit together.

After dinner, the MC told the simple story of Tim's coma. His dose of reality was designed to get the message across that

Tim had a lifelong disability, and we needed to raise as much money as possible.

Tim's parents stood bravely beside the podium. Frank was a St. Mary's Old Boy. In a month's time, his only son was meant to graduate. Something structural in my soul buckled under the weight of this reality. We wouldn't be graduating together. He might never walk or talk again.

Now, for the first time since the car crash, I sobbed uncontrollably in front of a public audience.

A dinner guest rubbed my shoulder. "You'll be okay."

No, I wouldn't be okay, and neither would Tim, insofar as *okay* meant being the way we were before.

• • • •

THE DAY BEFORE GRADUATION, Dom was charged with three counts of dangerous driving causing death and two counts of dangerous driving causing grievous bodily harm. The front page of the *Toowoomba Chronicle* was occupied by the latest twist in the tragedy.

I awoke with a head-splitting hangover, eyes bloodshot from a six-month diet of beer and tobacco, topped off with midnight binges of microwaved meat pies.

"You can't be late *today*," said my mother.

For thirteen years, I'd craved freedom from painful routines invented to prepare me for fifty years of gainful dissatisfaction. Now youth was a speedboat leaving the pier.

My parents kept up appearances for their final high-school graduation as legal guardians. Dad sported a tweed coat and a pair of speed-dealer sunglasses, a Band-Aid on his nose from another melanoma surgery. Mum wore pants and a loose cotton shirt. Her fingers were cocked for a quick cigarette on arrival.

"How about this weather?" she asked on the drive.

Dad grinned forgivingly at the UV rays that kept attempting to kill him. "Yep," he said. "It's a bloody ripper."

The ceremony was staged at St. Mary's new concrete cathedral. Clive Berghofer Arena was a gratuitously large basketball stadium funded by Toowoomba's richest right-wing millionaire, after the Catholic faculty supported his anti-recycled-water campaign.

The senior cohort of 2009 filed onto the stage in reverse alphabetical order. Plastic pews were crammed to capacity with families and seven hundred boys in navy ties and pale blue shirts.

"I want to mention a special person," said the principal, gesturing at the empty chair where my best friend was meant to be sitting. Our names were beside each other on the leadership board, but an invisible asterisk would affix itself to the house captain who didn't graduate.

I thought: DON'T CRY. Ever since I'd broken the seal of my tear ducts, I couldn't stop weeping in public. I collected plaques for topping English, English Extension, Modern History, Geography, and Drama, the most decorated pisswreck in the school. The principal testified to my *never-say-die* attitude in the face of adversity.

The graduates flowed beneath green emergency exit signs onto an oval yellow from drought, converging in a horde of white collars and sunburnt necks. In the absence of Tim, I led the final rendition of "When the Saints Go Marching In" alone. I flailed my limbs and strained my vocal cords. We all shoulder-charged one another with blunt force and ripped pockets from shirts that would never get washed or ironed again.

The moment of catharsis was followed by a civilized morning tea. Seniors wrote promises to stay in touch on each other's shirts with permanent marker, while parents entered into pissing contests about our career prospects.

The rest of the day was spent anticipating the best night of our lives: the Grade Twelve formal. Girls had invested in Brazilians, teeth whitening, tanning regimes, and thirty-day lemon detox diets. Some had become temporarily bulimic in an attempt to fit into a smaller dress size. Guys had aimed to make their bodies monumental, ripping pecs and lats and biceps at twenty-four-hour gym franchises, drinking protein shakes until their abs were visible.

I hadn't been so out of shape since I was an overweight kid, so I'd purchased a mirdle—a male girdle—on eBay to suppress my climbing BMI. After showering, I slipped into a tuxedo hired from Roger David, before tightening the bowtie around my neck like a noose.

"You'll be the most handsome man at the formal," said my mother, who wasn't coming due to "bad arthritis."

After collecting me, my father presented a hip flask of vodka from his blazer pocket. The silver flagon was specially imprinted with the worst year of my life: *2009*.

"Congratulations, mate," he said. "I'm so bloody proud of you. You're made of tougher stuff than me."

I was three beers deep when Frida arrived at the pre-drinks. It was the first time we'd seen each other since breaking up. She wore a white velvet dress. I introduced her to Dad and Hannah, my substitute mother.

Vincent's father had agreed to drop us at the formal in his black Mercedes-Benz. "*Lech Blaine*," said Frida. "Who knew you were so fancy?"

I opened the door. We held hands as she stepped inside. In the back seat, I swigged from a half-finished Corona.

"You look beautiful," I said.

"No funny business," she replied. "My lipstick is mint."

This left open the possibility of funny business after the formal. In the meantime, I tried valiantly to forget that we would be sitting at a makeshift table without Tim.

The route to the mock red carpet was blocked by a manu-factured traffic jam. A cavalcade of limousines, luxury sedans, convertibles, and hot rods ran five hundred yards up the main street. Traffic attendants in hi-vis directed our sedan into the final stretch of gridlock. At the exit, police sirens sent a warning to any overexcited chauffeurs tempted to rev their engines too hard.

"Are you okay?" asked Frida.

"I'm fine," I said. "Why?"

"You look like you saw a ghost."

The black Mercedes hit the finish line. I leapt from the back seat, but forgot to open Frida's door.

She joined me. "Sorry," I whispered, my elbow locking clumsily with hers.

The red carpet was lined with faux paparazzi. Bystanders rubbernecked the glamour and humiliation: who looked the best, and who didn't. I grinned as my body froze in the after-glow of camera flashes.

Thankfully, we made it through to the lobby of the venue, Rumours, the site of my escapades as a thirteen-year-old pool champion. It was as if all the muscles had been sucked from my stomach, leaving nothing but a clutter of fighting spiders.

"I need to go to the bathroom," I said.

"We need to make our entrance," said Frida.

"Do it without me."

In the last stall of the male toilets, I suffered a gut-wrenching panic attack. Tears streamed down heated cheeks and onto the pleats of my hired shirt.

Keep your chin up, Dad would say, so I swallowed vodka from the hip flask. Then I blew my runny nose, splashed a red face with water, and made a comeback before the start of offi-cial proceedings.

Rumours had been a nightclub for horny speed freaks in the 1980s and 1990s. Nowhere else in town was large enough to host formals, so the owner rebranded the fading facility as a crematorium for teenage dreams.

I high-fived the jocks and made sober bystanders embarrassed about their reserve. My father and sister sat at the table with Frida. I flirted with all the dates except mine, terrified that her brown eyes would trigger a public panic attack.

I wasn't the only bachelor in the room suffering from performance anxiety. Bashful Catholic schoolboys with bulging Adam's apples had wasted money on colognes, tuxedos, and ambitious stockpiles of contraception, only to learn that they were still the same tongue-tied young men.

Before my post-dinner toast, I mixed Smirnoff into a glass of Coke. The son-of-a-gun public speaker didn't address his best mate's brain injury, or the newspaper story about criminal charges against Dom.

"If anyone's wondering why I can't stop smiling," I said, "it's because I was extremely nervous. So I pictured everyone in the audience naked! And then instead of frightened, I became extremely excited."

I did one last speech for guffaws among the students, and mutterings about my drunkenness at the teacher's table. They decided against staging an intervention.

After dessert, the graduates descended onto the floor for a first dance. I hijacked the microphone and implored the cover singer to play "Eagle Rock," again dropping my trousers during the chorus. The graduates of 2009 hooted with amusement while shooting footage on their smartphones. I concluded with a war cry.

we are we are we are who?
St. Mary's St. Mary's: blue-white-blue
B-R-O-T-H-E-R-S! BROTHERS!

Who was I? Who was I? *Who was I? I* was a danger to myself and a stranger to those around me.

During the last dance, Frida failed to materialise, and I learned that she'd gone home early, blaming a headache. Now I was lumbered with a familiar loneliness, and my hip flask was bone dry.

I decided to leave too. My father and I shook hands. Outside, I slammed the door to Hannah's car, and cried like a dying animal from the moment we exited the parking lot until the tires hit the driveway in Glenvale.

Grief was a daily exercise in failing to say the right things, then feeling those emotions only when everyone else had stopped paying attention—so not having anyone to show them to, or freaking people out when you did. I pushed away Hannah's comforting fingertips.

"Is this about Frida leaving?" she asked.

"Yeah," I lied, because where else did I start?

"There are plenty of other fish in the sea," she said.

My sister was missing the point: none of the other girls would save me either. I was too young to discover that the great bastard of bereavement was life's chief emotional experience.

You can fall out of love, but not out of grief.

• • • •

SCHOOLIES WEEK IS AUSTRALIA'S ANSWER to spring break. For seven days at the end of November, twenty thousand Queensland teenagers descend on Gold Coast beaches to consecrate the privilege of being young and free and rich enough to spend a small fortune on getting obliterated. It nearly killed me.

Surfers Paradise—the capital of the glitter strip—boasted the highest density of strip clubs in the country. Ethics were suspended, and every vice permitted for the right price. You could truly purge the disobedience from your system before the new restraints of degrees and apprenticeships.

I stayed with six mates at The Islander, a yellow-brick building with pink trimmings. Inside, the clashing themes of Hawaii and Nevada were mashed together. Downstairs was a neon-lit bar called Vegas in Paradise that offered an all-you-can-eat breakfast buffet for ten dollars. In the gaming lounge, wrinkled retirees and tattooed rednecks toasted with bottles in the after-glow of slot machine payouts. Through the tinted windows, half-naked teenagers sunbathed around the swimming pool, skin dappled by the shade of fake palm fronds.

The first day was a haze of premeditated anarchy. Big Red brought eight bottles of homebrew rum, which we nicknamed moonshine and mixed with ginger ale.

"*Jingle bells, jingle bells,*" we sang, "*the Mary's boys are here.*"

The Islander was warmly regarded by former Schoolies as the most lawless establishment. In the bedrooms, deodoriser veiled the smell of mould and cigarettes. The décor was straight from the crayon-coloured eighties. The decay had been airbrushed from the photos online, but the deception was easily forgiven.

After approximately ten standard drinks in the space of two hours, I started existing in the present tense, responding only to the breathing bodies within touching distance. I let Big Red shave my curls into a mullet.

"Let's go fucking mental!" I yelled. "Let's go fucking mental!"

We gravitated to the balconies, open cages that scraped the sky and exposed occupants to the thrilling risk of fatal injury. Each November, they became exhibition spaces for casual sexism as young men exercised the privilege of possessing penises.

"Tits out for the boys," we chanted.

"Dicks out for the chicks," the girls replied.

The well-endowed or mistakenly confident bared tits and dicks. We mimicked media footage of previous Schoolies. Girls in bikinis French-kissed. Oglers levelled smartphones towards scripted outbreaks of promiscuity. Weathered cameramen aimed lenses at breasts that would get pixellated for the six o'clock news.

Drinking games incited adrenaline and kinship and eventually oblivion. One of my roommates shotgunned five cans of pre-mixed vodka in under three minutes. "Scull, motherfucker!" we chanted, so he had no choice. The congregation he left behind was delirious, gasping at thin air, convinced we'd witnessed something historically significant.

Half-dressed girls on the opposite end of our floor invited us to join them. I decided to take the scenic route, lifting my clumsy body over the unstable balustrades and scooting across a series of fibreglass chambers labelled DANGER—DO NOT STEP. My death wish was already the worst-kept secret at Schoolies. I lingered on each of the five ledges for an extra few seconds, wringing out the public exposure for extra shrieks and applause.

It was too much even for Big Red. "Take it easy," he said.

"Don't be weak," I said.

I downed endless shots of Midori. Everything went fuzzy before browning out. I embarked on a solo tour of the hotel. You didn't need to knock on doors before entering—each unit was a different room at the same party.

I witnessed girls pissing in the fire escapes, footprints of shit in hallways, bong hits at tables, bathtubs filled with vomit, bottles hurled off balconies. Strangers crushed pills against iPhone screens with school IDs and sniffed lines through rolled-up pocket money.

"*Swinging through the trees with my dick in my hands,*" I sang, "*I'm a mean motherfucker: I'm a Mary's man!*"

Twilight turned to night. We began a mass evacuation from our ravaged hotel rooms, coursing inexorably towards Cavill Avenue. Before dark, it was a prosaic shopping plaza. After, it turned into a human zoo: a precinct of beer gardens, nightclubs, titty bars, and tattoo studios.

I walked haughtily amid a pack of new best friends, staring into a kaleidoscope of bright lights and beautiful bodies.

A checkpoint had been established between society and the enchanted sands at the end of Cavill Avenue. Schoolies were identifiable by fluorescent wristbands, sealed with metal clips so they couldn't be slipped off. The barcodes were duplicated on the fluoro lanyards around our necks. Inside was a permit displaying our name, face, and birthdate. Security guards herded us through a maze of chain-link cages emblazoned with ads for energy drinks.

The vista featured ten thousand creatures stampeding between stages a few hundred yards apart. Limbs slick with sweat flickered in military-strength strobes. We hissed and whistled at each other, stray animals in heat, emitting the universal mating language.

It was a ten-second recipe for disappearance. The speakers spread amnesia between attendees. All the specific dreads and regrets of a person's life were cancelled out by the loudness of the music and the manic energy of the crowd.

Over the next couple of hours, I thrashed around to the edge of physical collapse. Volunteers in front of the stages handed out free water bottles to the crowd. The secret scheme was to hydrate partygoers enough that they'd sober up.

Suddenly, I was rubbing shoulders with Henry. The long arms of his doppelgänger were wrapped around a blonde girl in jean shorts and a bikini top.

"What are you looking at?" he yelled.

His creeped-out Juliet giggled at me.

"Nothing," I whispered.

I retreated to the beach. The sky was purple with heat and electricity. On the far side of the stages was a quicksilver city conjured from thin air by real estate tycoons, and trafficked to gullible boomers as a new blueprint for immortality. A helicopter searched for someone in the late-night surf. The Pacific Ocean lapped at the blackness between the shore and horizon.

For an uncomfortably long time, I stared glumly at my fellow graduates kissing gleefully on the sand and pissing knee-deep into the sea, wondering what the hell was wrong with me, what it'd take to be recruited into this cult of carefree breathing, to be okay, *for fuck's sake*, just this one night, one week, one life.

The time flashed from a grey skyscraper. It was quarter to ten on the first night of a seven-day bender. The only people I wanted to see were either dead or in the hospital. I headed for the exit, careful not to kick sand on any teenagers getting hand jobs.

Everything that glittered earlier on Cavill Avenue had turned to shit. Riot police patrolled opposing mobs, armed with pepper spray and tasers. Plainclothes cops slammed pill pushers into the back seats of unmarked cars. Paramedics fixed victims with stomach pumps and suture kits. News crews did laps of the plaza, waiting patiently for the violence they helped foment.

Young men came to Schoolies primed to emulate fights they'd seen on YouTube. Those who didn't know how to throw fists prepared to get their supple faces caved in by the rough knuckles of grown men. I saw a Schoolie get stretchered away while his attacker was shoved into a paddy wagon. Eyewitnesses shrieked like hyenas, sending footage to each other via Bluetooth. "Suck shit!" one shouted. The others laughed hysterically.

I arrived back at The Islander and showed my lanyard to the security guard. In the lobby, three Red Frogs accosted me. They were undercover religious evangelists scattered throughout the strip offering sweets and pancakes to sinners.

"Hi, buddy," said the leader. "Are you all right?"

I stared at him with a blank expression and walked to the lifts, which were stranded at the upper levels, so I climbed nine flights of stairs to a vandalised apartment.

On the balcony, a flatscreen TV was wrapped in a bedsheet. Kid Cudi's "Day 'n' Nite" vibrated between tall condos. The smell of pot fused with spew on the sea-salt breeze. The streets echoed with high-pitched voices promising to kill and screw each other indiscriminately. I watched the tiny outlines of the undead clusters I had just fled without a shred of lust or envy.

You can only bluff for so long. Now, in the midst of systematic bliss, I experienced the realisation that no number of nights like these, blinded by alcohol and dopamine, could ever change what had happened on May 2. And I didn't want to negotiate the matter on a twenty-four-hour suicide hotline or over free pancakes with sympathetic virgins in the hotel lobby.

I leaned against the rusted balustrades and concentrated on the bitumen nine floors down, a dead man wavering.

I looked away. I looked back again. I looked away. I looked back again. Then the door of the battered apartment swung open, laughter drifting down the hallway towards oblivion and beyond. I turned around and shut the shattered sliding door behind me.

Fast Nights, Dark Days

I N THE OPENING WEEKS OF SUMMER, I relocated to the big city: Brisbane. My sister and her boyfriend had found a two-bedroom unit in Woolloongabba for the three of us.

"This is a fresh start," said Hannah.

The heat in Brisbane had a deeper intensity. On a subtropical Tuesday morning, I threw out my cigarettes and weighed myself on the scales at the drugstore. The machine printed a receipt of my physical statistics. My BMI sat at 28.4. This put me deep inside the *overweight* category, eating steadily towards *obese*.

I put two sixty-tablet packets of FatBlaster MAX into the shopping basket and added three flavours of the FatBlaster ULTIMATE MAX Diet Shake: Dutch chocolate, cappuccino, and vanilla ice cream. The boxes were covered with dieting mantras.

REDUCE BODY FAT / BURN FAT / HELP CONTROL HUNGER

I filled a shopping cart with forty assorted cans of flavoured tuna. From the freezer I grabbed five packets of frozen vegetables. Dinner for the next three months would be three ounces of fish with five ounces of microwaved veggies, topped by a handful of sunflower seeds. My meals were tallied on a website called CalorieKing.

At Jetts Fitness, I signed the membership forms before embarking on a tour of the premises with a beefcake named Angus, whose Maori-inspired sleeve tattoo tapered off just above an Anglo forearm.

"You're gonna kill it," he said. "I can just tell. You want it bad. Some people don't want it badly enough. How bad do you want it?"

"Pretty bad," I said.

Angus sized up my soft body with contagious excitement. "Picture your rig in three months," he said. "Don't stop seeing it. Believe what you see. It's yours. More *you* than you. Ya know?"

I wanted more than a six-pack. Trauma has two rival desires: death and perfection. I planned to temporarily vanish and emerge a brand-new person, released from the secret burden of my lethal urges.

Each morning, I promptly consumed two huge maroon ovals of caffeine, before walking to a local café and buying a double-shot skinny flat white, and then entering my weight into an Excel spreadsheet. In two weeks, I went from 183.4 to 173.3, a loss of over ten pounds.

At the gym, I warmed up on the treadmill for ten minutes, increasing the speed and gradient every sixty seconds. This was followed by five minutes ripping my legs and shoulders to shreds on the rowing machine. Next, I spent half an hour pushing and pulling weights with my arms, shoulders, and chest. I did three reps of ten, increasing the heft as the weeks multiplied.

I finished with half an hour on the exercise bike before driving home, acutely unaware of who I was, apart from basics like where I lived. Dieting narrowed my focus to the only scenario I could control: calories in, calories out.

On my off day from the gym, I went for a walk. I started short: forty to fifty minutes. But soon enough I was gaining distance and speed. Afterwards, I stirred sachets of orange Hydralyte into soda water with a fork. The electrolytes and vitamin C mixed innovatively with the brain freezes and dehydration, delivering me, briefly, to a griefless present.

"You're going to get skin cancer," said Hannah.

To pay the rent, I got a job as a delivery driver for a gourmet pizza franchise. I travelled ballistically across upmarket suburbs where consumers required caviar and prosciutto to justify the consumption of junk food. Clients tipped me generously for speeding, not that I needed bribing. I chased premonitions of collisions and savoured the adrenaline rush of evading them.

By New Year's Day, I was 167.1 pounds. By February 1, I was 153.2 pounds. I ate less, exercised more, and fasted longer. Pretty soon there were no off days, just blank sequences between waking up, exercising, delivering pizzas, and passing out.

On the Saturday morning before Orientation Week, I caught a bus to Queen Street Mall and bought a new wardrobe with my life savings. I got skinny cream chinos and a canvas tote from Country Road. Two Ralph Lauren button-ups. A Ben Sherman polo. Wrangler jeans. Two Tommy Hilfiger T-shirts. R.M.Williams boots and a brown belt. Black Ray-Bans.

On the Monday of Orientation Week, I glided onto the leafy campus, a bogan incognito, and secured an internship with Kevin Rudd—the current prime minister—in my first politics lecture.

To satisfy her parents, Frida was studying piano at the Conservatorium. In my dehydrated daydreams, Frida and I shared brilliant opinions over coffee before steamy sex in her dorm room; I surged to a seat in parliament by age thirty.

I finally ran into Frida outside the library. She was with a group of strangers, and looked visibly hungover from an event at her prestigious college.

"Hey, Frida," I said.

"Lech?" she said.

We hugged without tenderness. She seemed more concerned than aroused by my appearance.

"Have you been eating?" she asked.

"I need to get to class," I said, even though I didn't have any classes left that day. "Great to see you."

That night, I delivered pizzas while wired on diet pills. Thin white lines blinked down a flat black strip.

• • • •

THE PROBLEM WITH RUNNING AWAY all the time was eventually I arrived somewhere. Each day, the bus to uni stopped at the Princess Alexandra Hospital. Once or twice a week, I pressed the red button to visit Tim.

I didn't realise the hotly contested nature of his convalescence. Last November, doctors had been prepared to write him off, because his bed could be dedicated to someone with better recovery prospects. Tim's family fought to gain him a place in the rehabilitation unit.

Now he was starting to repay their hope with slow improvements. He still couldn't walk or talk, but was able to write profane messages on a speech board—such as PUCK YOU, LECH, a reference to the sitcom *Summer Heights High*.

This was unfathomable to me: Tim could type my name, but not say it. So many broken dreams were left unspoken. Yet there was no vocabulary to acknowledge what he'd lost without diminishing his continuing existence.

"Puck you too," I replied.

We spent the majority of the visits playing Connect 4. I planned to make the games competitive before letting Tim win, until I realised that I had no say in the matter.

"I'll come back soon," I promised, but I never came back soon enough to alleviate the guilt that I felt after passing the hospital without pressing the red button.

I began to suffer recurring dreams about Tim. The year before, we had co-captained our house to victory at the swimming carnival, held at an aquatic centre called Milne Bay. Tim was a gifted swimmer. I wasn't. He secured crucial points in the pool while I led chants in the grandstand. After we raised the trophy, he tackled me, fully clothed, into the deep end. Lungfuls of laughter released a jet stream of bubbles through the chlorine.

In the nightmares, Tim sat beside the outside lane in a wheelchair. He begged me to dump him in the deep end. The grandstand cheered wildly. So I did it. Tim plunged to the bottom of the pool. The crowd went silent. The only person who could save his life was me. But I was paralysed by my survival instincts.

I woke up choking for breath and drenched in sweat, like I'd been bench-pressing the weight of the world with my skull. There was no going back to bed with a dread that heavy, so I scrolled aimlessly through Facebook until daybreak. I carried these deadweight dreams just beneath my suntanned skin throughout the first, fragile months of my DIY reinvention.

On weekends, I got blackout drunk at parties with outrageous themes. The next day, I spent hours adjusting the contrast of the photos to show myself in the happiest light. I monitored my iPhone for notifications, acutely addicted to the red flares of involuntary approval.

"Are you feeling all right?" asked Hannah.

"Never felt better," I said.

• • • •

THE FIRST ANNIVERSARY of the car crash caught me by surprise. I didn't have May 2 circled in my diary or set as a reminder on my iPhone. It was on the Sunday of that ominous long weekend. I knew, dimly, about memorial events planned in Toowoomba. I cited assignment deadlines and unmissable shifts.

On Saturday night, the steep streets were darkened by over-hanging fruit trees. I bitterly contemplated sleep—not as a genuine prospect, but more like an unfeasible overseas holiday.

The only way to untwist my corkscrew thoughts was to keep accelerating. Alongside the river, I hit a peak in the bend at high speed. Headlights ignited across the unlit bitumen. I didn't collide with the vehicle opposite, but I couldn't say with conviction that was a positive thing.

The narrator provided directions to the next address.

AT THE ROUNDABOUT, TAKE THE SECOND EXIT.

YOU HAVE ARRIVED AT YOUR DESTINATION.

The place had a rendered fence and sensor lights, and an intercom with a little camera. The customer answered the door as if he wasn't expecting me. Polo shirt and cologne. Fifties by the fistful.

"Hey, champ," he said. "Busy night or what?"

"Yep," I said. "Makes the time go quicker."

"That's the spirit. What's the damage?"

My dissociation had found a potential benefactor. I recited his order with premeditated glee. He grimaced. "I tell ya what, you don't bloody miss. Do ya?"

I grinned at him. The man gave me two fifties. Then he handed back a twenty from the change. "Buy yourself a six-pack."

"Thanks, mate," I said. "Have a good one!"

The hardest part of the shift was finishing. There was nowhere left to go except an empty apartment, because my sister and her boyfriend were back in Toowoomba for the long weekend, along with most of my friends.

Tonight, the eve of the anniversary, Facebook filled with people confessing to deep grief over the loss of Will, Hamish, and Henry. *Rest in peace*, they wrote. I thumbed through the condolences and the cheerful photos of the grievers who posted them. Their secret was the same as mine. A subterranean pain lurked below our curated profiles.

When I ran out of mourners to stalk, I moved on to the mourned. Unlike in a cemetery, I could see the bodies of the dead and spot new pictures they were missing from.

I searched my name on Google and consumed the old newspaper articles, fingering through the outrage and conspiracy theories in the comments. I studied the bloody images unproductively. I pressed my fingers against the pixels and kept scrolling and staring and scrolling.

Will, Hamish, and Henry were dead. I felt like a psychopath, ashamed that I could eat breakfast, brush my teeth, and smile at strangers on public transport. Meanwhile, my friends were gone, their families broken.

How was I capable of thinking about anything else?

It was 4:00 AM. I slid the door open to the balcony. Banks paid vast sums to plaster the city skyline with elegant logos, so that we'd dream about their life insurance plans. A survivor was stuck outside of time, always plummeting back towards the lone event that mattered, the only fuck worth giving.

Guilt about happiness. Guilt about sadness. Guilt about feeling guilt. Guilt about *not* feeling guilt. There was never any happy or unhappy medium. I either felt too messed up or not messed up enough.

• • • •

THE REST OF May never happened to me. I was fading away, finally, my brain and body forfeiting to the patient onslaught of trauma. Wide, low tides of irritation. Slow, scathing thoughts.

Staying in bed would betray a troubled state of mind to my sister, so I wasted entire days staging fruitless visits to university. The handsome campus ignited a fretting sense of decay. I did laps of the lake, head brimming with grim spirits, dodging brush turkeys and bin chickens, battered by the soundtrack of birdcalls and iPhone notifications.

I ignored the *please explain* emails from teachers and flaked on social activities. Classes and parties were light-years away from the skin-and-bone debates of my inner monologue. How was I supposed to write three-thousand-word essays on the theoretical underpinnings of global diplomacy, or go to bars dressed in a toga?

Late afternoons, I caught the bus without pressing the red button. The number of days between my visits to Tim accrued to weeks, before I went the entire month of May without a pit stop at the hospital.

In my dreams, I went to parties with Will, Hamish, and Henry, laughing serenely, only to be reminded midway through the apparitions that they were dead. I heaved with gut-wrenching grief, unsure if I was awake or weeping in my sleep, but knowing that the revenants would disappear, and I wouldn't be going with them.

Waking up, I was crippled by episodes of sleep paralysis that left me mute and rigid. I was suffocated by the most excruciating weight, a swooning sense of ruination. Teeth clenched. Head revving like a V-8 engine.

After finally breaking free, I vibrated with the colliding urges of survivor's guilt: relieved to be awake, but ashamed—and afraid—to be alive.

This is how insomnia begins to seem like the lesser of two evils. My sleep disorder became an art form. Three hours had been shaved close to zero. I ignored emails from the prime minister's office asking about my no-shows, and flunked all of my mid-semester assessments.

It would've only taken a few emails to explain the situation and gain extensions. I never considered my anguish as a condition, or my eroding sanity as something that needed urgent sandbagging. No, I believed that *I* was the only person who could see the elusive truth behind the glee on social media. We were all sleepwalking towards a steep cliff. I misconstrued the chemical imbalance in my brain as existential X-ray vision.

Ironically, the only activity that I remained capable of was driving at high speeds delivering pizzas to stockbrokers and doctors. On the road, I reached a state of flow that had been lost from my slow, sad days.

"You have arrived at the destination," said the GPS unit.

• • • •

ON MY FIFTH NIGHT of no sleep, I rose from bed and packed light for a long drive. It was 3:00 AM on Saturday, and Vincent had asked me to give a speech at his eighteenth birthday party that night back in Toowoomba.

The elevator slipped me into the concrete garage. My car exited through the gates. St. Lucia's footpaths were unpopulated. Coronation Drive was lifeless. Sporadic taxis delivered partygoers to sleep. Even the most devout drinkers couldn't outlast me.

On the motorway, I steadied the red needle at 130 kilometres, or 80 miles, per hour. I slowed for the speed cameras—at the same spot everyone did—before flooring it, targeting adrenaline and receiving the shyest flutter of excitement.

At what velocity does grief disappear? In that haywire frame of mind, there was no difference between *now* and *then*, the past and the future, speeding and dreaming. I felt intensely connected to every memory, including ones I hadn't made yet, the perfect lives of my fantasies and all of the emergency-exit urges.

Evangelical churches spread the Gospel of Jesus to the wicked motorists of the Warrego Highway. Billboards delivered anti-abortion scriptures alongside directions to adult superstores. After religion, the most popular subject was car crashes.

STOP. REVIVE. SURVIVE.

IF YOU DRINK & DRIVE, YOU'RE A BLOODY IDIOT

HIGH CRASH ZONE. SLOW DOWN.

EVERY KM OVER IS A KILLER

Daylight seeped across the vegetable farms. Kangaroos were silhouetted on road signs. The Great Dividing Range was tapering shades of green and black and grey on the horizon. The peaks looked way too faded, like an oil painting finished in crayon.

The car slid into a tsunami of trees. Mist spread across the windshield. I snuck into Toowoomba, sharing the road with semitrailers.

I hadn't been back to visit Mum since moving out. Mazda licked at my feet. The clothesline was bare—my mother didn't have anyone left to do laundry for. A foster carer without kids was like a pianist with missing fingers.

Still the same early riser, she sat on the patio in a purple nightgown, cigarette burning in the groove of a plastic ashtray. "My baby boy!" she said, eyes lighting up with surprise. She hugged me eagerly and asked questions about my life in Brisbane that I could barely answer.

"I've been really busy," I said.

"I know. Of course you have."

"What brings you home?"

"I've got an eighteenth tonight. And I've missed you."

Mum laughed. "Now I know you're telling porky pies!"

I didn't know why I went there instead of somewhere else, except that everywhere else made me uncomfortable. Trauma wasa paradoxical combination of homesickness and homelessness.

Mum said, "Are you all right?"

"Yeah. I'm just tired from the drive."

I wasn't lying this time. I was profoundly exhausted, so drained that I couldn't keep my eyes open any longer.

Mum led me inside. I couldn't decipher what she was saying, but it sounded agreeable, so I nodded. I glided to the lounge room, where my mother had spent a thousand nights. She laid a quilt over my shattered body.

I woke up eight hours later. The country-music channel blared from a plastic stereo. I could hear Mum tapping at the keyboard. She tracked the lives of her absent children. In the comment threads of news articles, she argued in favour of legalising gay marriage and eradicating local outbreaks of stray cats.

Mum saw me stirring in the black mirror of the TV. "Good afternoon, sleeping beauty," she said. "Coffee?"

"Please," I said.

"Are you sure everything is okay?"

"Yeah. Why wouldn't it be?"

"No reason."

Human beings find creative ways not to speak about the pains that plague us. So many skeletons. Where did I start? Our lives as we knew them were over: her marriage, my youth. We hadn't found convincing enough illusions to replace the old ones, or a vocabulary to convey the loneliness of losing those illusions.

In the late afternoon, before Vincent's party, I had a shower and shaved the glint of insomnia from my skin. Objectively, I'd never been more physically attractive.

Mum kissed me. "I hope you have the best time."

At Vincent's mansion, I parked my car between gum trees. Inside was a gathering of the close friends I'd been skilfully avoiding since the start of a nervous breakdown.

"Surprise!" I said.

I reciprocated handshakes and hugs. Everyone kept saying my full name: LECH BLAINE. The girls kissed my cheeks with real feeling. The guys cloaked their care with macho jokes.

"What rock have you been hiding under?"

"Who is this guy? I don't recognise him..."

"When was the last time you had a feed?"

"It's from all the fucking he's been doing."

I grinned convincingly. When the falsehoods came, I didn't recognise the confidence in my own voice. "I've been great! Heaps on my plate. Hitting the books. Hitting the gym."

I was cursed to spend my life pretending to be okay for an audience whose adoration I found confusing. They loved me unconditionally for the same reason I couldn't live with myself: I survived. Now I wanted to give back the winning raffle ticket.

The next five hours disappeared. I made a well-received speech before I became too incoherent. Vincent hugged me. "Thanks for coming, mate," he said. I drank at the same speed as high school, double-pumping beers and dropping Jäger-bombs, but I was thirty pounds lighter now, a featherweight climbing into the wrong boxing ring.

I entertained the crowd in Frida's vicinity, taking satisfaction from the glances I attracted. But by the time I was confident enough to approach her, I was so drunk that I could barely string a sentence together.

"You should slow down," she said.

"Are you playing hard to get?"

"I'm not a fan of Lech Blaine these days," she said, reminding me of Nick's accusation that I had changed.

Her lips pursed sympathetically. My sense of rejection registered twice: at high speed, and in slow motion.

"I've gotta take a piss," I said.

I walked around the side of the house. The music and carefree conversations filtered away. I pickpocketed the car keys from my own pants, outwitting any final moments of self-restraint.

I did a lap of the floodlit flag at Picnic Point and skidded downhill towards the city. Hidden by tinted windows, I emerged onto the main strip. Five sets of traffic lights rose in a narrow triangle. The road twinkled red and green like a Christmas tree.

A drunken mob swamped the pedestrian crossing alongside the Strand Theatre, where I had taken Frida to see *Disgrace*. I stopped at a pedestrian crossing. Men twitched with testosterone. Women gawked at them, lips round and red like laughing clowns.

I drove over the railway line. Grand Central Shopping Centre rose immense and empty on my left. A big yellow *M* glowed on my right. I pulled a swift U-turn and bounced over three speedbumps.

"Welcome to McDonald's!"

I requested a Double Quarter Pounder, a Big Mac, and a Filet-O-Fish with large fries. The teenage employee smiled at me with a transactional happiness. I waited five minutes for him to carry over a full paper bag.

"Thanks, mate," I mumbled. "Have a good one."

I hoped that I'd never quite arrive at my mother's house, that the journey would become a bubble I could drive inside forever. I took a detour through the one-way car park of an elite girls' school, weaving around speedbumps. A glow-in-the-dark sign showed a red cross stencilled over a right turn. Headlights approached on the left. They were far enough away for me to safely complete the illegal manoeuvre.

Sirens exploded in the rear-view mirror. I nearly shat myself. A *bad bad bad* adrenaline rush. I swerved into the first driveway and yanked the seat adjuster so that my body was flush below the line of the window.

The sirens stopped. My motor kept running. Footsteps thudded on the concrete. A flashlight beam scanned across my shut eyelids. Knuckles rapped against the glass. I opened my eyes slowly. The shadowy face of a police officer stared through the window, which I wound down.

"Have you had anything to drink tonight?"

"Nah," I said. "I've just been sleeping."

"How long have you been asleep?"

"All afternoon. Six hours, maybe. I was tired."

"I saw you make an illegal turn. Were you asleep then?"

"That wasn't me."

"I can smell alcohol on your breath."

"I had a few before I went to bed."

A middle-aged woman in a nightgown flew from a nearby front door. "I've been sleeping," I said. "Tell him. Tell him!"

The police officer told the frightened woman that everything was under control. He directed me to step from the vehicle, and said it didn't matter whether I'd been sleeping or not—the keys were in the ignition, so legally speaking I was in control of the vehicle.

I, the drunk insomniac, was outraged. "You can't arrest people for sleeping!"

"I'm not arresting you. Yet."

The officer pulled a breathalyser from his belt and unwrapped a mouthpiece from plastic. "Keep blowing until I tell you to stop," he said.

The machine sucked up my rank breath. One long hum was followed by a beep that sounded unpromising.

"You've provided a high-range alcohol reading," he said. "I'm placing you under arrest for the purpose of further analysis."

The cop opened the back door of his police car. A sheet of plexiglass divided authority from the shit-kickers.

We glided smoothly towards the city centre. The officer made a series of garbled remarks into the two-way. He stared in the rear-view mirror, grim with recognition. "You're the boy from the car crash," he said. "The one who walked away. Aren't you?"

I shrugged.

We pulled up outside the silver police station. I'd been here six times in twelve months to defend Dom from the accusation of dangerous driving.

I stumbled through the sliding doors and sat down inside a small, square room, waiting to be tested by a more precise piece of machinery. I needed to blow 0.00 per cent.

The computer whirred for thirty seconds before returning the dreadful verdict: 0.217 per cent. I could already see the headline: CAR CRASH SURVIVOR CAUGHT DRUNK DRIVING.

First, I was required to spend the night in lock-up. A young woman and an old man were on night shift. The guy sighed. "Anyone you want to call?"

"No," I said.

"Parents?"

I shook my head.

The girl took an inventory of my personal details. "Do you suffer from any mental health conditions?"

"I've got depression," I said.

I'd never said the word out loud, but it seemed like the only crisp way to label my unrequited desire to die.

The officers performed a strip search. They made me put any loose belongings into a clear plastic bag.

"Can I keep my phone?" I asked.

"No way."

Everything went inside. Wallet, iPhone, car keys, and digital camera. The bag was placed in a large plastic tub like the ones at the airport, along with my belt and shoes.

"You were in the Highfields crash," said the old cop.

I nodded. There was a mortifying silence.

"What were you doing behind the wheel of a car that pissed?"

We walked towards my jail cell. "I'm sorry," I said.

The man unlocked the door and handed me a freshly pressed prison blanket. "I've got one golden rule in life: don't apologise unless you know what you're sorry for."

The cell was deliberately unwelcoming. In the corner was a metal shitter with a missing seat. I took a sip of lukewarm water from the silver fountain. "Oi, ya weak dog," whispered the neighbouring deadbeat.

A red dot blinked from the security camera in the top corner of the cubicle. On the wall was a sign: YOU ARE CONSTANTLY BEING WATCHED. As if I didn't know this piece of wisdom already. It was advice to live and smile and die by.

"Fuck you, ya dog," growled my unseen adversary.

"Shut up, cunt," barked the guy beside him.

I lay stiff on the rigid surface, using the blanket as a makeshift pillow. I transitioned between the first two phases of grief: denial that I'd done anything wrong, and anger at the police for arresting me.

These delusions were entrées to the bottomless dish of depression that wrenched my insides apart from midnight until morning. I cried quietly to avoid being humiliated by the lunatics in the adjacent cells.

I canvassed all the ways I could kill myself once I was released, before conceding that I probably didn't have enough courage to follow through with any. So I planned elaborate vanishing acts. I'd withdraw all my money from an ATM. Throw my iPhone and car keys into the river. Buy clippers from a drugstore. Board a bus to Victoria.

A police officer opened the door. "You're free to leave," she said. I followed her to the front desk and signed the bail documents. I was served with a high-range DUI that immediately disqualified me from driving. My court appearance was set for three weeks' time.

The guy behind me was one of my dad's former customers. "Your old man's gonna be pissed," he said.

Outside, it was a beautiful June morning. Opportunistic taxi drivers waited across the road to intercept the brawlers and drunk drivers emerging from lock-up. The radio announced that an eighteen-year-old male had been arrested after providing a homicidally high breath test. I scrolled through the pictures of Vincent's party on my phone, scrutinising my grinning face for clues.

• • • •

DYING IS THE SECRET WISH of the survivor. I don't just mean by suicide, although that had become the most attractive exit strategy. I'm talking about the need for danger. The impulse to shipwreck the miracle of being alive.

On the Sunday night following my arrest, I committed social media suicide before doing anything too rash.

My regret kept intensifying as I slowly sobered up. Laughter floated over the back fence from a barbeque.

There were more obstacles to killing my Facebook account than throwing my body off a bridge or swallowing a fistful of sleeping pills. The jilted algorithm identified Will, Hamish, and Henry as my three best Facebook friends, because I'd spent the previous year stalking their digital apparitions. Images of us together were deployed to prevent me from taking the leap. They were going to miss me. Why was I betraying them?

My departure from social media had a bureaucratic euphemism: DEACTIVATION. The profile could be resurrected whenever the urge returned. I clicked *deactivate*. It didn't do much. I spent another sleepless night more adrift than normal.

The only thing I knew for sure was that I deserved death more than my friends, that my survival was a waste of breath. I was perfectly prepared to trade my life for theirs. *Why them? Why not me?* The midnight appeals went unanimously against me.

YOU SHOULD BE DEAD YOU SHOULD BE DEAD

I was beyond sleep, beyond study, beyond love, beyond wasting my breath and blood much longer.

My father pulled up in the driveway. I knew on a tenuous level that it must be Monday afternoon. A hushed argument ensued between former spouses at the other end of the house. I opened the door to hear my mother say, "He isn't playing silly buggers, Thomas. I'm worried he's going to hurt himself."

Dad's heavy steps proceeded up the long hallway. Coins clanged against keys in deep trouser pockets. He knocked softly on my bedroom door. I made him bang more urgently before I answered with pretend sleepiness.

"What's up?" I asked.

"It's me," he said.

I opened the door and wiped fake sleep from my eyes.

"G'day, big fella," he said. "Come and have a yarn."

I followed him out to the back patio. My father had sold the tavern a month earlier and was in the midst of a lawn bowls bender. I could've been about to receive a lecture or the rendition of a dirty joke.

"How'd you go at bowls?" I asked.

"Shit hot," he said, chuffed with himself, before remembering what he was here for. "So I spoke to my solicitor. He sang the praises of a criminal barrister. Best in the business. We'll go in tomorrow. He said to bring your report cards from school."

"Thanks," I said. "I appreciate it."

"How are ya feeling?"

"Struggling a bit."

"Fair enough. Your mum told me you want to quit uni."

I couldn't tell if he was angry or sympathetic.

"Yeah. Just for the rest of the year."

I could see he wanted more detail, but I begrudged his interest now that my life was over.

"Do whatever you need," he said. "I'll back you to the hilt."

"Thanks," I said.

"Don't mention it."

"I won't," I said, more ungratefully this time.

We talked awkwardly about everything except *why* I needed a lawyer: sport, the weather, his desire to renovate my childhood home and buy a motel up north.

"Lech Blaine," he said.

"Yep."

"What's the go?"

"What do you mean?"

Dad twisted his moustache. He was sixty, hair finally starting to recede, but still with ridiculously thick facial hair. "I can tell when you're beating around the bush," he said.

"I'm just tired."

"Well, I'm a bit bloody worried about ya."

"You're worried?"

"Yeah. So's your mother."

His disappearance and her alcoholism hit me as if they'd both happened a minute ago. I mustered all the courage I had left to hurt the person I needed more than anyone.

"It's a bit late for your *worry*," I said. "My life is fucked."

Dad looked like he'd been bitten by a green ant—wildly irritated that something so little could pack such a poisonous sting. "Oi," he said. "What's that supposed to mean?"

The moment grew both large and small, fast and slow. I gasped, slumping into my father's arms. But I couldn't cry, a symptom of my constipated emotional state.

Dad yanked me back towards him like a bouncer, nuzzling a sunburnt nose against my ear, stubble scraping against smooth skin. "What is it, mate?" he asked. "Tell me what the hell's going on."

"I can't."

My father laughed heartily. He lifted my chin with his fingers.

"You'll get through this. We all make mistakes. I've been done drunk driving. Bob Hawke was an alcoholic! He fixed his act up, and the country loved him. There's no use crying over spilt milk."

I twitched with anger at the missed clues, the constant comparisons with famous larrikins, his insistence that everything would be fine if I just continued to lift my dipping chin. "I want to kill myself," I said. "And you're still worried about whether or not I'll become the fucking prime minister!"

Dad studied my lightless eyes, finally recognising the tight deadline. So much heat and history flowed between us. He bit on a chapped, quivering lip. "Don't say that!" he said. "You're not going anywhere. Do you understand how much people love you? How much I love you?"

"It's too much to live with," I said.

"I can't lose you, mate," he said, weeping freely over me.

I hoped nothing would interrupt, that I could bottle up the thickening intimacy between us and live inside of it.

"Do you think I don't blame myself?" he asked.

"I'm sorry, Dad."

"Don't be sorry," he said. "Just don't kill yourself. I guarantee ya, mate: it's gonna get better. In twelve months' time you'll wonder what all the fuss was about."

"What about Tim?" I said. "He isn't improving."

My father's tenderness flickered with trademark irritation. "So you'll do him a favour by committing suicide? That's gonna do wonders for his recovery."

The tears began to dry. I could see a game plan whirring behind his eyes, the old coach stirring up. "I've done a pretty piss-poor job," he said. "But you can't keep all this shit to yourself. It's too much for one person."

The Survivor

"Just because you have stopped sinking doesn't mean you're not still underwater."

AMY HEMPEL

Solidarity
Forever

O N TUESDAY MORNING, I quit my pizza delivery job
and dropped out of university. My father and I drove
to Brisbane to collect my belongings, and straight back
to my childhood home in Mort Estate, which he'd received in
the peace treaty with my mother.

"Welcome to the Ritz!" he said. "There are only two rules:
no drugs, and don't shit where you eat or sleep."

"That's three rules," I said.

"You get the drift."

Twelve years after we left Mort Estate, Glenvale had been
infiltrated by violent meth dealers, while the inner-city slum of
my childhood was undergoing a renaissance thanks to gentrifi-
ers flooding back from the suburbs.

Our house remained dilapidated. Floorboards were covered
by linoleum, putrid shades of lime and ivory. The bedrooms
had seaweed-coloured carpet. In exchange for Dad paying my
exorbitant legal costs, I would help him complete an overdue
facelift.

"I don't need to give you a tour," he said.

My father's interior design principles gave the impression
that we were criminals hiding out after an art heist. There were

less than ten items of furniture, but at least fifty pieces of sports memorabilia, taped in bubble wrap to protect from scuff marks, and covered with blankets to hide them from burglars.

Bananas decorated the card table. The bar fridge contained milk, a tub of butter, a loaf of raisin bread, and a carton of Diet Coke. A stack of frozen dinners sat in the mini freezer. On that first night, two bachelors at a loose end played blackjack while eating Mongolian beef and sweet-and-sour pork.

"It's time for you to knuckle down," Dad said.

I had an appointment the next day with Dr. Rattray, my childhood GP. Still unable to sleep due to anxiety, I spent the night trawling the internet, becoming an iPhone psychiatrist. *Grief* was too universal. *Depression* didn't have enough teeth. So, using a series of free quizzes, I diagnosed myself with PTSD, bipolar II, alcoholism, social anxiety, and narcissistic personality disorder.

I didn't give my father the bad news yet. "All the best," he said the next morning, handing over a Mastercard.

Dr. Rattray's office sat opposite my primary school. In the waiting room, I rated twenty-two vague statements on a scale from 0 for NOT AT ALL to 4 for A LOT, according to my feelings about the car crash.

I think about it multiple times a day. I feel numb when I think about it. I know I have a lot of feelings about it, but I bury them.

A total of 44 or over indicated severe emotional disturbance. My score was 57.

The second survey included forty-two statements to help refine a diagnosis. Twenty-four received the maximum rating, including *I feel I am worthless; I feel I have nothing to look forward to; I can't experience any positive feeling;* and *I feel that life is meaningless.*

The cheerful receptionist tallied the grim results.

"Young Lech!" said Dr. Rattray when he emerged from his office. "You're a picture of health."

I shuffled into his office, unnerved by how delighted he was to see me. There was a tan line on his ring finger. Maybe he knew a thing or two about a rough trot.

"You don't seem happy to see me," he said. "What's up?"

I confessed to my arrest. Then, for the first time, I went into graphic detail about the daylight fatigue and midnight insomnia leading to a public act of self-destructiveness, and my peaking temptation to act on months of rising suicidal ideation.

"I've been reading about Freud's theory of the death drive," I said. "Repetition compulsion is making me re-enact the original source of trauma."

"Well, we don't have a tablet for *that*," said Dr. Rattray.

"I'm also inclined to suspect bipolar II or PTSD," I said, stung by his flippancy. "Although the frequent hypomanic tendencies—such as the grandiosity and impulsivity—could be evidence of narcissistic personality disorder."

The doctor sipped from a water bottle and reviewed the test results on a clipboard. My depression was *extremely severe*, but my stress and anxiety levels merely *severe*. I had no physical symptoms of PTSD, such as trembling hands or involuntary flashbacks, and no evidence of mania. The doctor smirked as if to say: *You think* this *is a mental breakdown?*

"You'd be the first self-diagnosed narcissist in the history of psychiatry!" he said. "But you sure don't love yourself much."

I was irritated. He seemed to be underestimating the record-breaking nature of my pain. I relitigated the case for a diagnosis of PTSD and bipolar II.

Dr. Rattray straightened his glasses. "I don't get the PTSD vibe," he said. "You started driving again straight after the car crash. All your nightmares are about missing dead friends, not the collision itself. And I'm sorry to tell you, my friend: drunk driving isn't a symptom of bipolar."

"So what's the problem then?" I said.

"Your biggest issue is that you haven't really grieved since the crash," he said. "What you need to do is work through the time-consuming business of understanding who you are and what you lost. Whereas I get the impression today that you want the most godawful diagnosis to give you a great excuse for the magistrate."

"That's not true! I'm taking full responsibility. But it's not the real me. Why else would I drive while drunk?"

"My theory? I think you climbed behind the wheel of a car for much the same reason you jumped into the passenger seat a year ago. To prove you are a man."

Dr. Rattray didn't have a cure for toxic masculinity, but he prescribed 50 milligrams of Pristiq as a short-term salve for suicidal ideation. His letter to a psychologist destroyed the soothing illusion that I was irredeemably cursed, and nothing I did would make a difference.

Mr. Blaine has a tendency to pathologise sadness that is produced by personality traits consistent since childhood, or the logical grief from witnessing the death of three close friends. He needs to learn coping mechanisms to process negative emotions, rather than numbing them with alcohol. I feel that generally the severity of symptoms is in keeping with the lesser diagnosis of an Adjustment Disorder (Reactive Depression).

On the way home I googled "famous writers with an adjustment disorder," but came up empty. The diagnosis was a crushing blow to the self-importance of my sorrow.

That afternoon, in a kitchen straight from the 1950s, I lost my pharmaceutical virginity to a serotonin–norepinephrine reuptake inhibitor. School students shrieked on their way home. The pink tablet went down with water from a corrugated tank. I felt an ancient pain uprooting from my long-suffering soul—or maybe that was just the taste of rust triggering déjà vu.

. . . .

THE FOLLOWING FEW WEEKS were like a combination of a home renovation show and *Dr. Phil*. On the first morning, when I sheepishly appeared for duty, Dad laughed at my Tommy Hilfiger T-shirt and ripped skinny jeans. "Put on some shorts, mate. We're not here to fuck spiders."

In the 1960s, my father had owned a house-painting business with his brother George. Now Dad delivered a tutorial about stripping wallpaper, refusing to take the easy way out and hire a steamer from the hardware store.

We saturated plasterboards with a foolproof concoction of hot water and a white powder, waiting for the material to soak through so we could remove it with scrapers. I imagined that ripping down the wallpaper would be akin to unwrapping Christmas presents. It was more like trying to remove permanent marker from a whiteboard with a tissue and spit—and each room contained five whiteboards brimming with black felt pen.

"Come on, ya mongrel!" my wifebeater-wearing father grunted while dripping with sweat, as if we were shearing sheep in one of my mother's favourite Banjo Paterson poems.

Low-slung footy shorts revealed the purple bruise running from hamstring to hip. The origin story of those permanently burst blood vessels had changed repeatedly over the years. Sometimes one of his sisters had pushed him off a moving truck. Other occasions it had happened when he was a pro wrestler, or a soldier in Vietnam. I could never get a serious answer.

"How did you actually break your hip?" I asked, deciding that he owed me some sincerity for the grit.

"It was a meatworks injury," he said. "I've told you that."

"Plus a million other things."

"Bloody hell then," he said. "Strap yourself in."

My father was the youngest of eleven siblings, and the first educated past primary school. He attended Bremer State High on a scholarship and displayed a natural aptitude for mathematics. "Back in those days, you didn't need a university degree for a good job. I could've got a cadetship at the bank with my grades."

Pop Blaine was unimpressed with those white-collar flights of fancy. *A banker! Don't be a wanker, Tommy.* Grade Eight became Dad's matriculation. A *real job* was secured at the abattoir.

Inside the slaughterhouse, carcasses swung from an overhead line. My father spent his weekdays wielding a knife from a raised concrete platform. The accident happened when he was sixteen, almost the same age I was in the car crash. He slipped on blood and shit from the eviscerated animals, and fell eight feet directly onto his hip. A shattered pelvis broke the skin like a hot knife through butter.

"It was so horrific," he said, "that I couldn't really feel anything for a few minutes. And then I just started howling from the agony."

At the public hospital, an infection nearly killed him. He spent six months convalescing. Dad's six adoring sisters plied him with a constant stream of comfort food: meat pies, sausage rolls, potato bakes. He packed on forty pounds, and a gammy leg ended up two inches shorter than the other.

"And that's when Allan Langer was born," he said. "End of July. I was in the surgery ward; your Auntie Rita was in the maternity ward. The circle of life!"

Unable to run, Dad retired from rugby league, and resigned himself to sports such as darts, pool, golf, and bowls. The high-school dropout couldn't wear a white collar due to a lack of education. This was how he became a jack-of-all-trades: not due to entrepreneurship, but as a means of survival.

Dad went into business with George. George was a great housepainter; Dad was brilliant with figures. But they couldn't keep the band together without wanting to kill each other. Dad accused him of being too loose with money; George called him a pencil-pushing skirt.

Dad quit. He bought a petrol station, then a news agency, then a taxi, doing well enough for himself, but not as well as Uncle George, who became a millionaire through the painting business my father deserted.

"That prick was kissed on the dick by good luck," he said.

I realised that Dad had been *me*. He was the underwhelming youngest son, a self-loathing benchwarmer, compensating for deep inferiority with crippling ambitions. We both coveted the love of a tough father and the respect of older brothers, due to a sly envy hiding behind all the piss-takes and mythmaking bluster.

• • • •

THAT NIGHT, DAD WATCHED *Who Wants to Be a Millionaire?* followed by the news. In my bedroom, I read *Self-Portrait in a Convex Mirror* by John Ashbery, whose work was recommended by the musician and poet David Berman.

> *The soul establishes itself.*
> *But how far can it swim through the eyes*
> *And still return safely to its nest?*

Most of the time, I had no idea what Ashbery was going on about—not unlike the blundering drunks at the pub when I was growing up, whose non sequiturs I had pretended to understand. But even Ashbery's gibberish made more sense than the bland, linear bullshit emitting from the TV.

The prevalence of those gray flakes falling?
They are sun motes. You have slept in the sun
Longer than the sphinx, and are none the wiser for it.

I couldn't imagine anything nobler than baffling the world with poetry. Yet I'd wasted so much stress and spit cloaking myself as a down-to-earth bloke.

The next day, I returned to the wallpaper with a vengeance.

"Sounds like George gave you a hard time," I said.

My father chuckled. "Yeah, he was a hard bastard."

"Is that why you gave me such a hard time?" I asked.

My father's eyes shot sideways from the wallpaper, brows furrowing to the bridge of his nose. "Give you a hard time... What did *you* get a hard time about?"

I offered the first example that came to mind: at the age of six, when I announced my retirement from swimming after the second lesson. He told me that I needed to be more like my brothers.

"It wasn't a personal preference," I said. "I couldn't swim."

"Mate, take my word for it. We fostered kids with brain damage who had more of a dig at swimming backstroke than you did."

I spent the next few hours stripping the wallpaper with a productive hostility. Silently, I pored over all the times after I quit playing football that my father petitioned me to "have a go" and stop spending all my spare time reading books and listening to music.

"You hated the fact that I wasn't Steven," I said.

Dad had listened to the thesis of fatherly bastardry with mostly dubious amusement until the invocation of my older brother. "You're kidding, aren't ya? I named you after Lech Wałęsa. *You* wanted to be the rugby league star."

"That would've been the only way to get your attention."

"What a crock of shit."

"When did you ever encourage me to be creative?"

"I bought you an acoustic guitar. Wasted all that money on piano lessons. Begged you to join the school musicals. To be creative. But in a team! You wanted to be the star of the show. Or you pulled the pin."

An unreliable narrator was learning how two people can have different interpretations of the same event, how we can translate identical languages into love or pain depending on point of view. Emotions can't be trusted as far as you can throw them.

"Deadset," he said. "You could read the *Sydney Morning Herald* front to back as a nine-year-old."

"Why wasn't that enough?" I asked.

"It was more than enough for me."

Dad confessed to worrying that my foster siblings would interpret as favouritism the biological son being allowed to quit if he wasn't gifted at something.

"It's all right to be ordinary, too. Like your father."

"I don't think you're ordinary," I said.

"I don't need you to pump my tires up, buddy. I've just never understood why you went to war with yourself."

"What do you mean?"

"You can read books and still watch sport. It's a piece of piss."

My puberty was spent deciding which identity was the real me and which the alter ego. The artist saw the larrikin as a shallow socialite. The larrikin saw the artist as a miserable elitist. Why did I need to pick sides?

• • • •

IT TOOK THREE DAYS to strip the house of wallpaper, and roughly the same amount of time to cover it with two fresh coats of paint.

"Now we're cooking with gas," Dad said.

Using a Stanley knife, we carved lino into squares. Then we heated the patches with a hairdryer, before excising them with scrapers.

Underneath the lino were impenetrable layers of papier-mâché that had been left to harden for five decades, a booby trap to test the mental fortitude of the money-hungry gentrifier who tried to remove it. Blaine & Son dedicated two days to removing the stubborn substance with bucketloads of toxic chemicals.

"Come on, you bastard," my father grumbled in the sunroom.

My father and I were nearly finished: all that needed to be done by my court appearance was varnishing the timber floors.

On a Thursday evening in the final week of June, a cabal of trade unionists and Labor Party powerbrokers met for dinner in the nation's capital to stage a coup against the prime minister.

Kevin Rudd—with whom I'd been interning until my nervous breakdown—was about to be replaced like old wallpaper by Julia Gillard, Australia's first female prime minister.

My father and I watched the world's first political uprising triggered by climate change, too excited for sleep. I was loyal to Kevin Rudd. Dad sided with the trade unionists who ruthlessly replaced him. *"Solidarity forever!"* he sang over a Diet Coke. *"For the union makes us strong."*

"I'm not sure that jingle will win over swinging voters."

We went to bed after midnight and woke up later than usual. My father boiled a pot of tea. I made an instant coffee and watched Dad prick his finger for a blood glucose test.

"Well, I reckon Ruddy's seat might be coming up for preselection. You should throw your hat into the ring."

"Politics seems a bit meaningless at the moment."

What I meant was that I could no longer imagine repeating soundbites each day for five decades. In some form, my life would be dedicated to crystallising the complexity of existence, not denying it.

"Never say never," said my father.

"*Never*. My political career was over before it started."

"Is that because you got done for drunk driving?"

"Well, it doesn't look great on the résumé."

I confessed to my father I wanted to study literature if I went back to university, rather than scheming about the quickest way to win a safe seat.

"You don't need to be PM," he said. "Do whatever makes you want to wake up. Become a poet. Or a housepainter. But do *something*. Otherwise you'll lose the plot."

The confidence of his proclamation offended me.

"I've just been trying to stay alive," I said.

"Has it been *that* bad?" Dad asked.

"Honestly? Yesterday was the first day in a month that I haven't felt the impulse to flog your car and drive it into the quarry."

"I'm happy you didn't," he said. "Not just because I *love* that car. You've still got the world at your feet."

"I don't think you can relate to what I've been through."

"That's not true."

For morning tea, Dad made raisin toast. Talk radio was blowing up. Professional chauvinists had begun their campaign of outrage against a female PM.

"I lost my parents a few years apart," he said.

"Yeah, I know that."

Dad occasionally alluded to the death of his parents. But I'd never known my mother's parents either, so his orphanhood didn't seem unusual to me, just one more unfortunate aspect of growing up without money.

"Dad was stronger than an ox," he said. "Big blacksmith hands. Could've killed people with them. But he never laid a finger on us kids."

My father studied outstretched palms. Hands that seemed so huge to me were now revealed as puny in his eyes.

"What about your mum?" I asked.

"Oh, I got some good floggings from her! She was a tough old girl. But soft on the inside. I was the youngest, so I got a lot of love." My father put down his toast, face distorted by anguish. "I was thirteen when she kicked the bucket. Way too young to see something like that."

"What happened?" I asked.

"Let's have a cuppa," he said.

Dad poured two cups, while telling me how one of his mum's ingrown toenails had become badly infected, as if the contamination had happened last week, not five decades ago. "Last thing she said was, 'I might not have a big toe when you come home from school, Tommy. Take one last look before you go.'"

At the hospital, during the routine procedure, her already volatile blood pressure went through the roof. She suffered a brain hemorrhage, blood dissolving every memory from two world wars and sixteen childbirths.

"Me and your Auntie Lil went to the ward that afternoon after school. Your Nan was a vegetable. So they stitched a metal clip through her tongue and lip to stop her from choking. We just watched her drip in a pool of drool and shit till she gave up."

That Friday was the dawn of unprecedented vulnerability. At the halfway mark of a boom that turned blacksmiths and meatworkers into real estate investors, Australia had a doomed new prime minister, triggering a decade of leadership coups. Meanwhile, I saw through a thick crust to the source of my father's toughness.

"I was shell-shocked, if I'm honest," he said. "Then the old man started losing it. He'd burst into my room after midnight. Drag me to the front steps. 'Good news, me little mate!' he'd say. 'Your mum's coming home!'"

"Was he drunk?" I asked.

"Nope. Didn't touch a drop of grog. All in his head."

Dad suffered the injury at the meatworks three years later. He was sentenced to six months' detention a floor above the ward where his mother died. Then Pop suffered major kidney failure, and died downstairs from his crippled son.

"I wanted the doctors to just keep pumping me with more drugs until all that pain went away," said my father. "So don't tell me I don't know what it's like."

The death of his parents meant working eighty hours a week to keep at bay his existential dread. Real estate was about his only biological child and what might one day become mine, so that I'd never get left with nothing.

My father's public openness and private unknowability had always puzzled me. I'd been too young to appreciate how a man can spend five decades steadying himself against the dead. I understood him now, the heir to his aloofness. We kept people at a distance for dear life, so that it hurt less if they disappeared.

"Life's not perfect," he said. "But it's a million times better than killin' yourself. That's like comparing stepping on chewing gum to stepping in dog shit."

A year after wishing he was out of his misery, Dad's oldest brother, Jack, the new patriarch of the family, died of a heart attack at thirty-nine. My father had lost his mother, father, and brother in the space of five years.

And then, like in a Hollywood movie, he won the lottery. He limped into the news agency, fresh from getting the pins in his hip removed, and bought a Golden Casket ticket. The next day, there was no disputing the matching numbers on his docket.

My father splurged on a 1968 Ford Falcon sedan and put the rest in savings, a nest egg that would grow large enough for him to buy a petrol station.

"It was the happiest day of my life," he said. "Until you were born, of course. I picked up your Auntie Lil in this gleaming gold XT Falcon. Six-pack between us."

My father grinned as if his foot was still on the accelerator, before realising that it was an unsuitable happy-ever-after for a car crash survivor charged with drunk driving.

"My point is luck. I don't believe anything happens for a reason. But I trust math. And the law of averages."

"That's the thing," I said. "I won the lottery just by being alive."

My father pondered that line of thinking, before smiling at me, locating a nearby specimen for his thesis about loss and luck: *I* was his counterargument to killing myself.

"Luck doesn't happen just once," he said.

I grew dizzy from six hours of huffing paint fumes while discovering history's hidden repetitions, muffled by the human capacity for miscommunication.

"So you're saying I should buy a lotto ticket?" I asked.

"What I'm saying is that if you swim through shit creek for long enough, something is going to make it worth the effort. And sooner than you think, too."

Performance
Anxiety

O N A MONDAY MORNING, I faced the Toowoomba Magistrates Court. My startlingly calm criminal barrister riffled through my file.

"It's not bipolar?" he asked. "Or PTSD?"

"No," I said. "Just depression."

"I can work with depression."

We went over the narrative and possible sentences. I would most likely lose my licence for at least a year and receive a hefty fine, but might avoid a conviction.

The barrister put on his obligatory wig.

"Okay, it's showtime," he said.

Dad and I followed him up the courthouse steps. I put my wallet and iPhone into a plastic crate and held my breath as uninterested guards scanned for weapons with a metal detector. Most of us smuggled in nothing but the ugliness of experiences we wanted to flee from.

Inside, I reunited with my barrister, who was busy shaking hands with an array of current and former clients. That morning, the courthouse seemed to be filled with Dad's old customers. A drunk waved at us, sleeves of a hoodie raised to publicise the tattoo of a scorpion.

"Tommy!" he said. "We're both innocent, brother."

"Fuck me dead," my father muttered.

LECH BLAINE was one of the first names listed beside the courtroom. The magistrate presided over interchangeable human pains. "You've had a hard life," he said to a deaf driver caught behind the wheel twice in the same day. "But you seem determined to make life harder. Next time you'll be leaving in handcuffs."

When my case was called, the barrister gave a five-star performance attesting to my remorse. "This is a young man with a bright future dealt a bad hand by a tragic accident," he said. "Can anyone blame him for losing control of his life? He deserves a second chance."

The magistrate read references from former teachers and local politicians, along with Dr. Rattray's diagnosis. He agreed I was a fine young man of enormous potential who'd slipped off the rails.

"The aftermath of that car crash hasn't ended yet," he said. "It will go on for some time. But I hope that now you get the help that you so desperately need."

The justice system was designed to forgive white private-school boys like me. I was suspended from driving for six months and placed on probation for a year.

"No fine or conviction," said the magistrate.

I imagined screaming, *I'm guilty! I could've killed someone! Lock me up and throw away the key!*

"Thank you, Your Honour," I said.

Even the newspaper was sympathetic. It reported the court appearance alongside a photo from my interview after the car crash: *The court heard that Blaine was seeing a psychiatrist and medicated for depression. The magistrate said a number of character witnesses noted a change and the incident was out of character.*

My most objective character reference was the action I'd been arrested for. What I really wanted was official confirmation that Will, Hamish, and Henry deserved to be alive more than I did, but no one was going to give me that. And the ruling on Dom's guilt or innocence was still months away.

• • • •

BACK IN BRISBANE, I got a job as a waiter at Easts Leagues Club, a cathedral of slot machines. I committed to remaining sober for July, not in a social media stunt to raise money for charity, but to keep a promise to my probation officer. I needed to visit her at decreasing intervals for the next year.

"You want to know the common denominator for most of my clients—black, white, rich, poor?" she asked.

"What's that?"

"Getting on the grog," she said. "People like you could put people like me out of a job if you gave up drinking."

I nodded, while privately disagreeing. Sobriety reduced the likelihood of my pain spilling over into public display, but it didn't cure the underlying despair. In the short term, it sharpened it, because there were no distractions.

Another condition of probation was regular appointments with a psychologist. My sister—a high-achieving psychology student—organised free therapy with a decorated professor named Christopher. The only catch was that my confessions would be livestreamed to a theatre of graduate students.

I agreed to the innovative arrangement, and completed an exhaustive mood disorder quiz before the first session. Christopher wore a nice suit and expensive shoes. I'd located the antithesis of my stiff-lipped, single-syllable, thick-forearmed father. "Good afternoon, Lech," he said, gently shaking my hand. "It's delightful to meet you."

The sound engineer hooked up our microphones before disappearing. We skipped through the legal formalities. All of the aspiring shrinks a few rooms away had signed confidentiality agreements in order to glimpse the kaleidoscope of my soul.

"Do you have any questions?" asked Christopher.

"What technique are we using? CBT? Psychoanalysis?"

"I tend not to be that formal. Therapists use fancy labels to reassure themselves they know exactly what they are doing, when in reality we are working it out."

Despite a litany of degrees, Christopher had a practical approach to the science of the mind, seeing himself as more handyman than engineer. He wanted to start at the beginning. "This might seem unorthodox, but I don't want to speak about the traffic accident until we have a portrait of *who* you are. How did your parents meet?"

Over the next three sessions, I spontaneously narrated the oral version of "A Portrait of the Artist as a Young Larrikin." Towards the end of the third session, as I waxed lyrical about those moneyless and mostly unremembered years in the bush, my sentimentality became tinged with embarrassment.

"Sorry for getting nostalgic," I said. "I'm making my childhood sound like a Slim Dusty song."

"But you were clearly showered with affection."

"That's why my early childhood seems a bit irrelevant. Everyone treated me like I was God's gift."

"That's *why* it's important to explore. While gratifying at the time, I imagine the withdrawals must've been severe. The adoration couldn't last. But you knew how good it felt. So, naturally, you wanted to re-create that."

"Yeah," I said. "It was a blast!"

"This explains the soul-crushing desire for success."

"Well, yeah."

• • • •

THERAPY DREDGED UP a memory from my youth that I had repressed, until Christopher withdrew it brutally from my psyche. I was nine years old. My father paid me one dollar in the morning and two dollars at night to help open and close the corner store before and after school. One Saturday morning in spring, he played nervously with his handlebar moustache. "We need to have a chat, champion," he said, switching off the horseracing on the TV. This meant it must be serious.

I nodded, certain I was about to get a pay raise. Dad fetched me a cream soda from the fridge and himself a Diet Coke.

"I've decided to move away from Toowoomba," he said.

I was delighted by the news. During the 2000 Olympics, we did a road trip to Barcaldine, the birthplace of the Labor Party, to inspect a pub for sale. I wanted to be Dad's number two at an even bigger enterprise. It didn't concern me that Barcaldine was twelve hours away. "To B-B-Barcaldine?" I stuttered. "When are we m-m-moving?"

My father could hardly make eye contact. He talked to me as if we were bankrupt business partners, not father and son. "Unfortunately, you're not coming with me. Your mother wants to stay in Toowoomba. And I respect her decision. But I need a new business opportunity. This place could send us down the gurgler."

My father explained he had mortgages to pay, and the logistical difficulties of spending holidays with him in the bush, and the brutal reality that sometimes husbands and wives have different priorities in life.

Nothing he said to justify it mattered. The fact that he'd even contemplated leaving without me drove a dagger into my belief that the two of us were a history-making team.

"This is about your future," he said. "We can't go broke. Or you'll be eating baked beans from the tin for dinner every night."

"Who cares?" I said, eyes wet. "I love baked beans!"

"Baked beans are great," he said. "In moderation."

I went home and wailed in the mildewed sunroom. The canvas blinds cast bars of sunlight against the wallpaper, turning it into a prison cell.

"Baby," said my mother, running in. "What's the matter?"

I told her: Dad was taking off. We were getting left behind. A naive smile spread across Mum's face. Dad so frequently threatened to pack up his belongings and buy a rundown pub in the middle of nowhere—places like Charleville, Taroom, Julia Creek—that she had stopped taking his wanderlust seriously.

"He's pulling your leg," she said.

"Ask him!"

Mum called my father—three hundred yards away at the corner store—to confirm that I'd fallen for another of his convincing piss-takes.

"Your son's upset," she said. "He thinks that you're moving north."

She listened to the shopkeeper sternly clarify the gravity of the latest business proposition, which he'd leaked to me first. Chagrin was replaced with anguish. Mum couldn't speak, so deep was her sense of rejection from a man who inspired devotion by spreading his attention thin.

"Whatever happens," she said to me, "we'll be okay, baby."

I was an old head on young shoulders. "No, we won't."

My father's confirmation of the plan made me start wailing again, and now Mum was howling too. The timing didn't seem like a coincidence. John was about to graduate from high school, a year after Steven. Dad was leaving me behind with the female faction of the family, because I had a heart the size of a split pea.

That day, I wept like never before. Nothing that serious had ever happened to me. I figured that he might stick around if I stopped crying all the time and became more like my older brothers: tough guys with dry eyes and bulging biceps. "I'll do anything to make him stay!" I cried.

Dad didn't end up leaving for another six years. But the prospect of his rejection was an axe hovering above my heart. The character traits of a larrikin were minted into my sensitive soul by chasing the admiration of a larger-than-life father.

It was a major breakthrough. With the jury of postgraduate students, who I'd mostly forgotten were watching, Christopher and I analysed my intensifying allegiance to a brave patriarch over an anxious matriarch. This led to a coming of age that was both high-achieving and self-destructive.

"It sounds like you have no stable anchoring point about *who* you are," said Christopher. "Besides an underlying desire to be loved, especially by your father."

"I just want to stop relying on positive feedback."

"That's really been our overarching project here. Just being who you *are*, rather than performing an act."

Christopher didn't make me take an oath to tell the truth. That was the difference between a courtroom and his office: what mattered wasn't whether an event happened precisely as I remembered it, but the emotions it evoked.

"You love talking about your dad," said Christopher, "even negatively. But you struggle talking about your mum."

"I don't really think about her that much. She's got a drinking problem. We haven't connected for a long time."

Christopher listened to my blinkered interpretations, before countering them. "There is no stronger bond than the one between mother and child," he said. "I think you have repressed the excruciating pain of losing it. Especially when all of your other siblings missed the worst of her alcoholism."

• • • •

BY OCTOBER, the serotonin levels in my brain had consolidated after eighteen months of depletion, freefall, and sluggish recovery. My lows became higher and the highs longer, boosted by Pristiq, regular exercise, and weekly sessions with Christopher.

As we moved through my puberty, the emotional geologist excavated my deepest shames. I told him how I started watching porn at eleven. In Grade Eight, I reached third base before I could ejaculate, cementing sexual activity as both exhilarating and humiliating.

"So I don't know what the hell you call that," I said.

"Modern masculinity," said Christopher.

The only topic still more taboo for a young man than suicidal ideation was sexual dysfunction. With some discomfort, I confessed that I had struggled to enjoy sex with Frida and others, despite an adolescence spent furiously yearning to *fuck anything with a pulse*, as my father would say about John.

"You are describing a textbook case of performance anxiety," said Christopher.

"I'm no shrinking violet," I said. "I've just spent three months spilling my guts to a roomful of total strangers."

"The crucial difference is that you're not expecting any of my graduate students to love you."

Christopher listened to my history of grand romantic infatuations combined with consistent physical dissatisfaction, before offering a blunt synopsis of the underlying problem.

"Your sex life has become overlaid with all of those woeful emotional longings. You were trying to beat your brothers to the punch. Be admired as a real man by your father. And find substitute sources of love to your mother."

"What the fuck?" I said. "I'm definitely not thinking about any of them when I'm having sex with someone."

"Of course not. It's subconscious. But the physical pleasure of sex becomes an afterthought. In that moment of potential pleasure, you regress to a little boy, not a man. Adding a physical layer to a psychological shame."

I sat in silence for a few minutes, unable to make eye contact with Christopher, until nodding softly in defeat.

"You are petrified of getting rejected again," he said.

"Or maybe I haven't found true love."

"I'm not sure that's a prerequisite."

"So any hole is a goal? You *are* my father!"

"I don't want to advocate promiscuity, Lech. But you are eighteen. You can't re-create the romantic intensity of *Romeo and Juliet* with every girl you sleep with."

Christopher could see things that I remained in denial about. I wanted a crush to justify my existence.

• • • •

EVENTUALLY, WE ENTERED the final act. Christopher and I joined the dots between a larger-than-life little boy and the suicidal daredevil arrested for drunk driving. His students scrutinised my symptoms for clues to a diagnosis.

"How did you meet Tim?" he asked.

I introduced the other passengers in the order they appeared in my life, pretending that the narrator didn't know what was coming.

How did you meet Will?

How did you meet Hamish?

How did you meet Henry?

I was forced to recall their personalities and physical characteristics. I lamented the lost possibility of drifting amicably apart, flawed and forgetful men, untouched by trauma.

"I found this group of mates who embraced my weirdness, but still knew how to have a good time," I said. "And they were good people. Educated. Creative."

"They were boys you could relate to," said Christopher.

"Right. I didn't have any contradictions, because they hadn't known me since I was a kid. I wasn't a nerd or a jock. I was just smart and funny. And they loved me."

And so a psychologist with a DIY ethos deceived a highbrow survivor into grieving. The clichés of public tragedy had reduced my friends to abstract casualties. Christopher made them real to me again, by making me real to myself.

I confessed how I frequently wished, on a molecular level, that I could sacrifice my survival for theirs.

"Do you think about where they'd be now?" he asked.

"Never. What's the point? It is what it is."

"The accident wasn't inevitable," he said. "It will be incredibly painful. But I think you need to allow yourself to imagine what might have been. Or you'll never know what you lost that night."

My diagnosis was a let-down. The expert agreed with Dr. Rattray: I suffered from the universal mood disorder of being someone's son and brother, of loving too much and not getting enough love.

"We all exist on a spectrum," he said. "And you are closer to bipolar than the average person. But your emotions don't strike me as symptomatic of a chronic condition."

"What do they strike you as?"

"As revealing someone who is slightly more prone to sadness than the average person. But who is also more capable of creativity and compassion."

"That's comforting. But also really depressing."

"Why?"

"Because it feels like I'm never going to be cured of anything. This will just go on and on and on..."

"That's right!" he said with gleeful negativity. "It's the insuperable tragedy of human existence, really, isn't it? We are all stuck with who we are."

"Particularly me."

"I don't want to destroy your ego, Lech. But you are pretty normal. Take it from someone who knows."

I nodded, even though it sounded naive. But the more masks I saw behind in the years to come, the more I would realise that Christopher was right: everyone I knew was struggling against something huge and hidden. We are all haunted by past mistakes and heartbreaks, and trapped within the invisible prisons of our brain chemistry and DNA.

Unmotherly

NOBODY WAS TOO SURPRISED when my mother went insane. For years, my family had speculated about her topsy-turvy nerves like they were risky shares, always on the verge of going bust. But none of us did much to stop it from happening.

My mother's friend Ingrid called on a Thursday night in the middle of November to say that Mum had sent a series of paranoid emails and text messages: she had a theory that my father and John were plotting her murder and aiming to sell her house for a vast profit.

"I'm up at the hospital with your mother," said Ingrid. "To make sure that she hasn't been poisoned."

Ingrid, a qualified psychologist, had convinced my delusional mother to visit Emergency on the logic that the doctors could confirm if she'd actually been poisoned.

"She's having a mental breakdown," Ingrid whispered.

Hannah and I listened on loudspeaker to Mum interrupting Ingrid in a hostile voice. "Your father is up to something!" she shouted. "I'm top of his hit list!"

We called the apparent assassin, who'd just bought a three-star motel five hours away in Bundaberg. He had timed his exit from Toowoomba to perfection.

"That makes sense," he said. "She's been sending me the most bloody bizarre text messages. About how she's going to dig up all the buried money."

"You didn't think to mention that?" said Hannah.

"It cracked me up. I thought she was being funny."

Since Mum believed that her ex-husband and son wanted to kill her, neither was an appropriate caregiver. Hannah was in the middle of final-year exams. She had a pivotal assessment the following day. I had time on my hands, but no licence. It was 8:30 PM: too late for a Greyhound.

My sister offered a clear-eyed plan: I could find a friend who might provide a last-minute lift. If this wasn't possible, she would drive us herself and return to Brisbane the following morning, forgoing sleep.

I rang Vincent and explained in basic outline the family crisis.

"I'll come straight over," he said.

Vincent neglected to mention that he needed to drive back to Brisbane first thing the next morning for an exam. Twenty minutes later, he arrived in a blue vw and we hit the road. "So what's going on?" he asked.

I'd consistently rebuffed Vincent's offer of *someone to talk to*. But now I confessed to my mother's drinking problem, and the marriage breakdown precipitating a mental collapse. We talked about the aftermath of the car crash and my arrest for drunk driving. I told him about Christopher and the antidepressants.

"I never thought I'd see a shrink," I said. "But I'm actually starting to feel pretty good."

Vincent stared ahead. "I was on antidepressants for a bit."

"What?" I asked, as if to say: how could *you* be depressed? Vincent had seemingly so much to envy—a golden child from a rich family on the fast track to a productive adulthood. But he had suffered a post-Schoolies correction, he said, bottling up all his grief until after graduation. For a month, he barely left his room, cycling between day-long blankness and nightly crying fits.

"My mum was freaked out," he said. "The GP gave me a Prozac trial."

"Did it help?" I asked.

"I didn't really notice a difference after I stopped," he said. "But I probably wasn't *that* depressed. I think I just needed to process how fucked up that year was. So, for you . . . I can't, like, imagine it."

At the hospital, Vincent idled outside the sliding doors of Emergency. "Do you want me to come in?"

"Nah. Shit's probably about to hit the fan. But thanks for this. And for everything. I really do appreciate it. And needed it."

"Call me whenever."

Mum was in the waiting area, tired but wide-eyed, like someone three pills deep in a nightclub at 3:00 AM.

"Where's the money, honey?" she asked.

"I don't know about any money, Mum," I said.

My mother grinned at Ingrid with vindication. "See, I knew he would come! He's on my side. Not his father's. But not for a lack of trying: that bastard turned all my kids against me. But Lech's *mine*. Did you know that, Ingrid? He's mine."

I smiled at my mother until I couldn't fake it. Physically, she was diminishing. A gut hung above skinny legs, revealing no trace of feminine shape. Bloated cheeks topped sinking jowls.

For the next six hours, Ingrid and I maintained the charade that we were taking my mother for a general health check-up due to her insomnia. We didn't disagree this might be a side effect of a poisoning attempt.

"People are finally listening!" she said. "All those years of being ignored. But I'm going to find the money. I don't even *believe* in money! But the greed of the man . . ."

Around 4:00 AM, my mother was finally ushered into one of the observation rooms. The doctor asked the enthusiastic subject to recite the day, month, and year; her date of birth; the name of the prime minister.

Frustratingly, my mother nailed the impromptu game of trivia. This gave the doctor confidence that she wasn't deranged enough to be committed to a psychiatric ward. We had a conversation in the hallway.

"You can't let her leave like this," I said.

"Unfortunately, she doesn't meet the threshold for an involuntary mental health order. But I can give her some medication to take the edge off."

The doctor provided Valium and temazepam, and a referral for a psychiatrist. We left as the sun was rising. Ingrid dropped us home. My mother swallowed the Valium with a glass of tap water. She chain-smoked beside the Jacuzzi for fifteen minutes. I sat at the computer in the poolroom.

"Lovely to see you," she mumbled while stumbling past.

I did an inventory of the liquor supplies. The fridge was filled with Bundaberg rum. My father's relinquished Scotch collection sat, dust-covered, in the rumpus room. I stockpiled the lot in a basket and hid it at the top of my old wardrobe in the granny flat.

The next day, I woke to find my mother frantically wringing out wet clothes in the laundry. It was the ritual of someone trying to cure insanity through routine.

"What a lovely surprise to have you back!" she said. "You never should have left. Free rent here. And I could do your washing for nothing if you mowed the lawn every once in a while. Think about it."

The hallway walls had been fleeced of family portraits, leaving only the outlines of frames. I found the missing pictures lined up on the kitchen bench. A hammer had been taken to my father's face. In a few, my mother had used scissors and glue to place my face over his. We looked like inbred siblings.

"Mum," I yelled. "Come here."

The hands of the vandal were wet from wringing.

"What the hell is this about?" I asked.

She reviewed her project, pleased. "Lech, he's out of my life. You're the only man I need now."

"Are you serious?"

"Deadly," she said, and went back to the laundry.

I swept up the shards of glass with a dustpan and brush, and sent my father an update. *the doctors don't reckon she's insane enough yet. but you'll be glad to know that she's taken a hammer to your photos*

better than to the head, he said.

good point, I wrote, and hid the hammer with the alcohol. I called Dr. Rattray and gave a blunt summary.

"She's been suffering from depression for a while," he said, "but I never knew that she was such a heavy drinker. How long has this been going on?"

I had no idea. My family had made a livelihood from bad drunks, who did shots of tequila before swearing at bartenders and vomiting on their feet. But Mum was a shy, medicinal alcoholic, seeking a sly solution to anxiety. Her drinking never produced outbreaks of anger or abuse.

"Seven years," I said. "Ten, maybe."

"Bring her in late this afternoon. I can see her after my regular appointments."

I found my mother hanging sheets from the clothesline.

"We're going to see Dr. Rattray later," I said.

"What for?" she asked.

"A team meeting."

I fell asleep in the granny flat. Late in the afternoon, a crazed guardian angel shook me awake.

"Where is it?" she asked.

I screwed up my face. "Where's what?"

I went into the kitchen. The fridge and cupboards were emptied. Shards of crockery glistened in the spilt milk.

"This is ridiculous! I'm a fifty-year-old woman!"

"I don't know what you're talking about."

Mum squeezed my wrists. "Tell me where it is. Now!"

I put my hands on sunken shoulders. "Come with me to the doctor," I said, "and I'll give it back to you."

"Do you promise?"

"I promise."

I called a taxi. Inside, she accused the cab driver of being a spy for my father. He kept a straight face to the interrogations. At the clinic, Dr. Rattray waited behind the counter. The receptionists had gone home.

"Lenore, what a lovely surprise," he said.

"Fuck off," she whispered. We went into the office and sat down. The doctor spoke slowly.

"Lenore, I think you need to go to the hospital. What do you reckon?"

"No! No, no, no, no, no!"

Mum muttered a foreign language of complaint, beads of sweat collecting on her forehead.

Dr. Rattray called for an ambulance, while typing up a mental health assessment order. The paramedics arrived quietly, without sirens. The matriarch was strapped to the gurney in the back of the van.

One of the paramedics was the mother of a girl I knew from high school. "You've had a tough eighteen months, haven't you?" she said as we arrived. "All the best with your mum."

"Thanks," I said.

Mum was delivered to the same consultation room where I learnt that Will was dead. I sat in that small, bright space with a sense of vindication. Contrary to the promises of optimists, one catastrophe had not stopped another from happening.

"Hello, Lenore," said the doctor. "Do you know what day it is today?"

Pure blankness.

"Can you tell me the name of your lovely son?"

My mother flunked the quiz. She gulped for breath, lock-jawed. Eyelids slid shut as sounds slipped from her lips. Then she collapsed onto the floor.

Back-up surged into the room. My mother was injected with sedatives. A nurse explained that radiologists would examine her body to confirm that there were no organic reasons for the delirium, such as a brain tumour or a blood clot—a matter-of-fact way of saying she might be terminally ill rather than clinically insane.

I didn't worry about calling Dad or Hannah until tomorrow. Mum wasn't going anywhere fast. I drifted to the taxi rank.

"One Evergreen Court, Glenvale, please," I said after a brain freeze.

"Too easy, mate," said the cab driver. "Long day, eh?"

"You wouldn't read about it," I said.

• • • •

MUM PASSED THE SCANS with flying colours. Her brain was free from tumour and hemorrhage. She didn't have a urinary tract infection. The patient was transferred to the psychiatric ward within a leafy section of the hospital.

I met with a doctor and a psychiatrist, shocked that I was old enough to take legal responsibility for a grown woman.

"A psychiatric diagnosis is a lot harder to pin down than a physical one," warned the doctor. But based on my field reports, and my mother's physical presentation at the hospital, the medical professionals had collaborated to make a prelim-inary diagnosis. "Wernicke-Korsakoff's syndrome," said the psychiatrist. He made it sound like a computer virus.

What it meant was that long-term drinking had inhibited my mother's intake of thiamine. The deficiency had reached a critical level. Unlike a computer, much of the damage was irreversible. Many sufferers of the syndrome ended up in care facilities.

One benefit of a breakdown was that the hospital could try to sandbag as much of her sanity as possible.

"This could be a positive thing," said the doctor.

A nurse led me down the hallways with an access card. Awards for good behaviour hung along the walls, as in a kindergarten. The door was marked with an initial: *L. Blaine*, the same as mine. I hesitated, picturing my mother strapped against a mattress in a straitjacket.

Inside, a daytime soap opera played on a wall-mounted television. She slurped yogurt with a dessert spoon.

"Hello, baby," she said. "When are we going home?"

"Not yet. How are you feeling?"

"Great! Unlike your father's, my body is in excellent shape."

When the credits rolled, Mum pressed a buzzer to call the nurse back. She grabbed some pens and an A4 notepad.

Outside, we sat in a gazebo.

"I've worked it all out," she said.

Mum assembled the sheets into a flow chart. Each page was covered in immaculate handwriting.

"Everything makes sense," she said.

The schema was incomprehensible. "Not exactly."

Mum gestured to take a closer look. It was a tree of her life from birth to adulthood, she explained, charting links between luck and loss, chance and catastrophe. I didn't recognise most of the names or dates. A red cross indicated catastrophe. The pages were covered with red crosses.

One phrase was rewritten in undulating flourishes. It said, *WE BEGIN AGAIN OVER AND OVER AND OVER.*

Her face grew lucid. "Everything's already happened."

We sat quietly until a nurse arrived to take her back inside.

Before I left, my mother provided a shopping list of urgently required items: liquorice allsorts, underwear, and a carton of menthol cigarettes.

"Bring them back by dinnertime," she said. "Don't forget."

I was led down a different hallway to the exit. Near the front station, the doors to the rooms featured small squares of shatterproof glass. Some of them filled with vacant gazes as we walked past. The nurse answered a question that I wasn't going to ask. "The harder cases."

I walked into a stagnant afternoon. There was nowhere to go, so I did laps of the hospital grounds. The people arriving were too stricken to see me. The people leaving saw everything. They smiled without flashing teeth.

I remembered the day I left for Brisbane. In the rear-view mirror, a loving mother had waved glumly at a reluctant son.

I'd split her in two: the tender bookworm she'd been when I was a child, and the burden of nerves she'd become. If I'd looked closer, or knew what to look for, I might've seen more signs. Mostly, I was too shaken by shame to admit that her problem was mine.

• • • •

MY MOTHER WAS in the psych ward for a fortnight. It is both inspiring and terrifying how quickly the brain of a psychiatric patient can return to legal functionality.

"I'm better than before," she said.

Her exams over, Hannah did most of the negotiations with the hospital to end the involuntary treatment order. Mum was discharged on the proviso that someone else live at home, at least for the summer. So I quit my job and moved in with her. A social worker visited once a week. Meals on Wheels delivered lunch and dinner.

"I should have a nervous breakdown more often," said my mother, grinning at the tinfoil containers.

My mother's licence was suspended. Dr. Rattray sent a letter to the Department of Transport and Main Roads stating that she was a danger behind the wheel, based on intelligence from Hannah.

Mum blamed my sensible sister for stranding us in the suburbs. "Your sister's a snitch!" she said. "Fancy complaining about *my* driving. There's nothing wrong with it. Is there?"

My mother had infamously got her licence by doing a driving test with the local copper in nearby Chinchilla. He had picked up a free carton of beer after taking the bartender's wife for a quick lap around a town without traffic lights.

"I reckon you're a fine driver," I said.

"Thank you, darling! I'm lucky that *you've* got my back."

As a bureaucratic olive branch, Main Roads provided a registration plate for a mobility scooter. I helped my mother select a model. Each morning, she flew to the news agency at the end of the cul-de-sac.

"Yahoo," she said. "I'm a real wild child!"

Soon, she was back to volunteering at the second-hand clothing store three days a week. I got a job at the Spotted Cow, which was patronised by local private-school alumni. During the day, I worked through Don DeLillo's oeuvre. At night, I poured craft beers and chardonnays for affluent alcoholics.

I walked to and from work, fifty minutes each way. Sometimes the return leg didn't start until after 3:00 AM. Tile turned to metal as I power-walked to Glenvale via Mort Estate. I was a nocturnal flaneur, fleeing from the slow burn of my own loneliness.

I woke up after lunch and swallowed a pink antidepressant without thinking, before having a Nescafé Blend 43 with Mum. Our exchanges grew more revealing. She asked about my mental health. I asked about hers. She admitted to missing my father with irrational passion.

"That doesn't sound irrational," I said. "You were married forever."

"Maybe I'm not that crazy," she said.

Summer seeped into spring. The death of another season triggered thick humidity and drought-breaking downpours. One sunny afternoon, my mother sat on the back patio drinking a can of Pepsi Max. The back lawn was reborn. I mowed and weed-whacked. Dried-up dog shits exploded into white puffs underneath the lawn mower.

"My beautiful baby," she said, clapping as if I was deactivating landmines. "You're bloody amazing!"

We found ways to braid our days with flickers of intimacy. It wasn't a slapstick family sitcom, or a cathartic outpouring. But we existed under the same roof without the tight-knit bitterness of my high-school years.

That December, uni students fled back to Toowoomba for the holidays. They arrived with wider vocabularies, waistlines, and repertoires of sexual positions. Invitations for social gatherings leaked out online.

I missed most of the parties due to working the late shift at the Spotted Cow. Vincent updated me on the drunken hookups on Sunday afternoons.

"I'm having a party on New Year's Eve," he said.

"Damn. I'll be working. It's the busiest night of the year."

Vincent drove over to my house in Glenvale every second or third weekday. We went for grocery trips, picking up the sweets and Pepsi Max that my mother kept secret from her dietician.

"Thanks, Vincent," said Mum. "Lech's lucky to have a mate like you."

Vincent brought an acoustic guitar with him. We spent the start of the summer covering songs by Pavement and the Silver Jews. We tried to rewrite "Range Life" and "The Wild Kindness" with different chords and lyrics. I pictured tall, skinny Vincent

as Stephen Malkmus to my unkempt and sullen David Berman.
I replaced the lyrics I wrote in high school with the postmodern
poetry I'd been jotting down since leaving for university.

"No offence," said Vincent, trying to bring me gently back
to earth. "But your confessional lyrics are way better than the
cryptic shit."

"You just don't get it," I said.

"So nobody else will."

On Christmas Eve, Negative Gearing started recording
demos of a magnum opus called *Dark Side of the Boom*, an EP of
breakup songs. Vincent convinced me to sing in an Australian
accent rather than an American one.

after the party and into the darkness
half-cut but surprised by the starkness
of you pissing in the gutter of a street
on the dour edge of this town

Vincent tinkered with the feedback levels, grinning. "Frida's
coming on New Year's," he said. "You should call in sick."

"Those lyrics aren't about Frida," I said, blushing. "They're
about a girl I met in Brisbane."

"Sure."

"And even if they were about her, there's no way in hell that
Frida's going to get back with me. I'm a notorious criminal."

Vincent's amused expression grew serious. "Did you ever
ask Frida about *her* problems?" he said.

"What's that supposed to mean?"

"I just think sometimes you are so obsessed with covering
up your own shit that you ignore everyone else's," said Vincent.

It takes a minor miracle for someone to admit that none of
us has a clue what we're doing.

Crooked Rain, Crooked Rain

FOR CHRISTMAS THAT YEAR, Queenslanders received a freak weather event. Floodwaters spread north, south, east, and west, wiping out country towns. Looters were kept at bay by snakes and crocodiles. The prime minister sent Black Hawk helicopters. Nobody knew if this was truly necessary. Everyone agreed it was a noble gesture anyway.

On New Year's Eve, I was rostered on until 3:00 AM. But the Spotted Cow was empty after a week of unrelenting thunderstorms, and the owner let me leave at 7:00 PM. My licence had been reinstated a few days earlier. So I drove to Vincent's.

The sky was low and dark. The sound of laughter fluttered up to the balcony and mingled with mosquitoes buzzing above the drying gutters. Spectators watched a mixed-doubles tennis match below. Frida returned serve.

"Thanks for gracing us," said Vincent.

"I didn't want anyone to think I was dead."

We drank vodka punch and complained about the weather like retirees. I heard the word *muggy* twenty times in ten minutes.

Frida wore a white linen button-up tucked into denim shorts. She won in a tiebreaker, and came up to the balcony, hugging me unselfconsciously. "Mr. Blaine. Fancy seeing you here."

I couldn't think of anything profound to say. Frida touched my arm. "Are you having an aneurysm?" she asked.

"I don't think so. But I only want to die in your eyes."

"That's the most romantic thing you've ever said to me."

Frida and I spoke to other people before picking up our conversation. I didn't get so drunk that I couldn't speak in order to lessen the weight of anticipation.

"I see you reactivated Facebook," she said. "Sheep."

"I have a deep chemical dependency," I said.

"Why did you delete it then?"

"I was also having an existential crisis."

"Who isn't having an existential crisis?"

Frida was considering quitting the Conservatorium. Starring in small-town orchestras put her on the middle rung of serious musicians.

"There are pianists a lot better than me," she said.

We didn't run out of things to say, and the phrases we strung together tumbled out urgently, due to the sense that we were being upfront for once.

"Have you been seeing anyone?" she said.

"My psychologist. His name is Christopher."

I admitted to dropping out of university and moving home, assuming that she already knew the basics.

I can't remember what song was playing at midnight. Frida and I kissed for the first time since she broke up with me. We were oblivious to any spectators. Life had never happened that spontaneously before.

After another hour or so together, Frida led me to a spare bedroom. "I'm on the pill now," she said.

I tried not to imagine the previous beneficiaries of her prescription. We grinned at each other's bodies. She was all ass, hips, and limbs. I was skin and bone. Two naked teenagers rushed clumsily to save something that hadn't begun yet.

"Do you think that I'm more chilled out now?" I asked afterwards.

Frida kissed me on the cheek and chin and lips. "You'd have to be the least chilled-out person I've ever met. But that's great. Chill people put me to sleep."

• • • •

ON NEW YEAR'S DAY, Frida and I rehydrated with mineral water in the kitchen of her empty manor. "Honey, I'm home!" the hostess shouted to the ghost of her parents. They were yachting across a foreign body of water. Outside, the sky was grey blanket. I synced my iPhone with the universal speakers and played Pavement's "Crooked Rain, Crooked Rain."

"Let's go for a swim!" said Frida, ditching a black bra and panties on the gate. We skinny-dipped before the deluge, doggy-paddling and kissing through the chlorine.

"What's your New Year's resolution?" she asked.

"To get super, super ripped."

Frida snorted loudly, throat seizing up with glee.

"Thanks for the vote of confidence," I said. "What's yours?"

"To lose ten pounds while eating and drinking like a pig. Which is more implausible than you getting buff."

Lightning creased the sky. We rushed back inside. In the shower, I watched droplets of water magnify the mole on Frida's cheek.

"I love your eyes," she said. "They change colour."

For afternoon tea, Frida slapped together a platter of vegetarian snacks. Spinach quiche with zucchini relish. Hummus and sourdough. Sundried tomatoes and pickled olives. Cheeses rippled with mould. It was a world away from my childhood staple of frozen meat pies.

I asked if the material on my fat-free cracker was apricot jam. Frida assumed I was joking. "It's quince paste, you dickhead," she said.

I mocked myself in a thick drawl. Irony was a defence against the fact that my uncouth ocker accent was largely authentic. "What do ya call this, *darl*?" I said, a reference to *The Castle*, an Australian comedy.

Frida squinted at me suspiciously. "Arancini balls."

"Yeah," I said. "But it's what you do with them!"

Frida hadn't seen *The Castle*, so the joke went over her head. She picked one up and threw it at me.

"I'm feeding you out of politeness," she said. "Not playing your sick fantasy of a housewife."

When we finished, I stacked the dishwasher and wiped down the benches. Frida's guardians watched me like hawks from the door of the fridge. I wondered if I could morph into their sophisticated future son-in-law.

"Do you want something from the fridge?" asked Frida.

"No. I'm just admiring. It's an absolute ripper!"

"You are passionate about the most niche details."

"That's where the magic is at," I said.

Midnight kisses and skinny-dipping at midday. The niche details don't deserve ellipsis. They are lifesaving.

• • • •

RAIN FELL SO THICKLY it looked digital. Frida stood at my bedroom window, one of Allan Langer's grass-stained Queensland jerseys hanging past her immaculate ass.

"What if it doesn't stop?" she asked.

I furrowed my brow and said, "It's gonna stop," pretending at conviction. But there were no gaps in the vista, just panel after panel of grey. Backyards were turning into channels of liquid and debris.

Our evacuation to my granny flat had been triggered by the arrival of Frida's parents. I resented that she still hadn't introduced me to them. Frida seemed irritated I wasn't taking the flood warnings seriously enough.

"We might need to leave," she said.

I raised my arms behind Frida. "I refuse to flee from a sinking ship! I will stay until the last home is taken!"

Frida's brow furrowed.

"We live on a mountain," I said. "It's not going to flood."

"And what if it does?"

"I'm not leaving for anything less than a tsunami."

Frida let my confidence hang for a few crucial beats. "I've noticed," she said. "You're not going *anywhere*."

"You'd rather watch the news."

"I'd rather have *sex*," said Frida. "But most of the time you'd rather read a novel than fuck me."

I was offended, not just for the searing critique of my libido, but on behalf of Don DeLillo's best sentences.

"I'd be more carefree if I grew up in Rangeville," I said.

"How many pubs has your dad owned?"

"Not enough to buy me a new VW."

Her bright eyes turned black. "You're a private-school boy from Toowoomba," she said. "Not a Sri Lankan refugee."

I smiled despite the prickle of self-pity in my throat.

Frida linked conciliatory fingers between mine. "What's up?" she asked.

Frida knew nothing about me, not really. I didn't want her to think that I was an oversensitive dickhead. I laid my insecurities on the table. "I'm just a little bit hurt that we had to come back to my place. As soon as your parents got back. Like you're hiding me from them."

Frida was irritated, then amused, then sorry for her amusement. "Is *that* why you're pissed off?"

"I know I'm not the boy next door."

"The only reason I haven't introduced you to my parents is because you've never introduced me to yours."

"Frida," I said. "My dad took off two years ago. Mum was an alcoholic. *Is* an alcoholic. Dry at the moment. She was in a psych ward six weeks ago."

Frida used my chest as an armrest. Her dark arms were covered with freckles and mosquito bites, souvenirs from summers past and present.

"I didn't know all that. And I'm sorry. But that doesn't mean you should keep her hidden away like a dark secret."

"It's humiliating."

"I can deal with it."

Frida recited a litany of family secrets, a tangled web of infidelities and addictions. She admitted to a general sense that she'd never be flawless enough for OCD parents and competitive frenemies.

That day, Frida performed an incredible act of mercy: she killed any fantasies I still had that she could fix me.

• • • •

FRIDA AND I SPENT Sunday night apart for the first time since New Year's Eve. I texted her. *Missing me yet?* When she didn't respond, I assumed the worst.

You're not going anywhere, Frida had said earlier.

I needed to do something besides working at a pub and drinking coffee with a recovering alcoholic. That's why on a monsoonal Monday afternoon, I slipped proof of my mother's disability pension into a plastic sleeve and set out for the welfare office, so that I could afford to return to Brisbane.

Streetlights shone at lunchtime. Roads gushed with rain. The shriek of fire engines had sounded less pressing as the wet weeks became inundated months.

I reached East Creek. Mud-coloured floodwater lapped at the bumpers of bureaucrats. I retreated, parked beside Hog's Breath Cafe, and ran towards the sliding doors of the social services office.

Henry's mother, Melissa, was behind the queue-less counter. Although I knew she worked there, I was still winded by seeing her.

"How are you, Lech?" she asked.

"I'm good," I said.

Melissa checked that I'd filled in the forms correctly.

"I saw you deleted Facebook," she said.

"I reactivated it the other day."

"Good. I like to know what you're up to."

I provided Melissa with a truncated version of my recovery from major depression, and the fresh decision to move back to Brisbane for university.

"What will you study?" she asked. "Politics?"

"English literature," I said. "Maybe creative writing."

"You should go for it. Henry always said that he thought you'd be some kind of writer. 'You should see the books in his room, Mum! All of us are looking at soft-porn magazines. Lech's too busy reading poetry.'"

The sound of Henry's name punctured my numbness.

"He really loved you, Lech. I hope you remember that."

"I know. He made me feel good about myself."

"Well, you deserve to feel good. We all do."

I submitted the application and kissed Melissa goodbye. Outside, matching fire engines wailed past. Bystanders cocked smartphones towards an uprooted tree. I retreated to the car.

Two thunderstorms had converged above the Pacific Ocean. A supercell flew inland so rapidly it outflanked warning systems. The wipers gnashed against the glass, unable to keep up. Red lights blinked. Police blocked traffic. I inched through white-knuckle gridlock. My iPhone still hadn't vibrated with a reply from Frida.

Once home, I rushed inside to watch the live disaster. During an ad break, my mother grabbed me a towel so I could dry off.

"Baby," she said. "Thank God you're okay! I was trying to call. The network must be down."

I realised that Frida hadn't received my message. The anchor kept referring to an *inland tsunami*. I looked outside, but I didn't see any tidal waves. A reporter waded through a flooded street, umbrella in shreds.

Vehicles parked beside East Creek rammed against each other like bumper cars. Antennas peeked from coffee-coloured froth. Water tanks, letterboxes, wheelie bins, metal containers, and showroom furniture joined a street parade of submarine rubbish.

"That could've been me," I said.

"You are the luckiest boy alive," said my mother.

We were interrupted by the jingle of breaking news. Footage showed a family marooned on the roof of a Mercedes-Benz at a familiar intersection. A forty-three-year-old woman and thirteen-year-old boy had been swept to their deaths, leaving an eleven-year-old boy behind. I blinked at the image of a drenched survivor clinging to a street sign. He would become the global face of a catastrophic summer.

"Hey, Lech," said my mother. "Are you all right?"

I told her about running into Henry's mother, and my decision to study literature.

"What's stopping you writing for a living?" she asked.

"There's no money in it," I said.

"There's also no money in being unhappy."

Later, when my mother went to bed, she kissed me good-night, no trace of rum on her breath.

"Sleep well, baby," she said. "*I love you.*"

• • • •

IT BECAME THE WETTEST WEEK in Queensland history. The politicians declared a state of emergency. Hardware stores ran out of flashlights and Swiss Army knives.

My mother's Meals on Wheels were delayed indefinitely. At the nearest shopping centre, squads of survivalist retirees jammed car trunks with milk, eggs, bread, and toilet paper from ransacked supermarkets.

I filled a trolley with baked beans, chili con carne, and frozen meat pies. Luckily, the one dessert still in the freezer was Neapolitan ice cream, Mum's favourite. I bought her two tubs, a block of chocolate, and a carton of Pepsi Max.

A black VW was in the carport when I arrived home. Two women were deep in conversation beside the mobility scooter. My mother wore a T-shirt, tracksuit pants, and flip-flops. Frida was in activewear and pink Asics.

"Your lovely girlfriend was just describing all the nice things you've told her about me," said my mother.

Frida laughed. My cheeks reddened.

"Sorry, darling," Mum said. "I just meant your friend who happens to be a girl. Where have you been hiding her?"

"G'day, Frida," I said. "I wasn't expecting you."

"I wanted to make sure you were alive!"

"She baked a carrot cake," said my mother.

"To celebrate our survival," said Frida.

We shuffled inside. I unpacked the supplies.

"Frida's neighbour said the Range could be closed for *months*," said my mother. "You might have to keep living here."

Frida saw the portrait of ten-year-old me on the fridge in a blue-and-white St. Mary's uniform.

"You were cute!" said Frida. "And gigantic."

"He wasn't much of an athlete."

"Thanks, Mum," I said.

Frida and I retreated to the separate granny flat. I turned on the television. The flood that flattened Toowoomba had travelled at high speed to Brisbane. Reporters chanted the words DEBRIS! and UNPRECEDENTED!

The township of Grantham had been obliterated. News crews filmed police choppers saving families from rooftops. Gutters sank underneath a mudslide. Twelve people had drowned.

We made out with the gravest possible concentration.

"Nothing like a flood to get the pulse racing," I said.

"*Now* you want to discuss the floods," said Frida.

The human race will be saved from extinction by horny teenagers fornicating in the face of death. Frida climaxed. I couldn't.

"Is this good for you?" she asked.

"It's fantastic!" I said. "Why do you ask?"

"It's been taking... a long time. Which I'm all for. But say if there's anything I can do. I won't be offended."

"I think it's a side effect of my antidepressants. But it doesn't matter if I don't come."

Frida synchronised my body to the bedroom with lips and fingertips. She guided me inside from behind.

"Don't think about anything," she said, "except how good this feels."

My orgasm felt better than a million piss shivers.

"That was the best thirty seconds of my life," I said.

"I can't be having all the fun," said Frida.

Frida didn't cure my depression, but she opened my eyes to a few little beauties that persisted in the wake of death. Falling asleep next to a warm body after slow sex. Making a person smile with their eyes shut in the grey light of a dawning day.

Frida proved that I wasn't excluded from these saving graces due to the painful things that I'd seen and done and dreamed.

• • • •

BACK IN BRISBANE, I moved into a three-bedroom unit with Vincent and Big Red. We had all graduated from different high schools and ideological traditions. Big Red grew up on a farm, the son of National Party voters, and wanted to be a professional rugby union player. Vincent, the son of white-collar Liberal Party voters, was studying law.

"How's the serenity?" asked Big Red, slurping a protein shake following an afternoon gym workout.

Vincent and I sipped from beers. On our sixth-floor balcony, we watched tiny cranes serenade the skyscrapers. Coronation Drive—sunk in the floods—was slowed by roadworks. Motorists pressed horns like they were morphine pumps.

"So much serenity," said Vincent.

In the afternoons, I scaled the rolling hills of St. Lucia, shirtless to avoid nipple chafe. Mud mapped flood levels on the balustrades of tall Queenslanders. Hard rubbish covered front lawns lush from summer inundations.

My father's new motel in Bundaberg was booming due to emergency workers staying for municipal repairs. He was running the business with a Maori barmaid from one of our pubs.

"It should flood more often!" he said on the phone.

"There's no use crying over spilt milk," I said.

"Make hay while the sun is shining, mate," he said.

I was studying English literature and creative writing, and getting high distinctions. But recovering from depression was like trying to unlearn a second language. My brain translated mundane frustrations into excruciating pains. Some days, a stubbed toe or missed bus seemed like the last straw.

"My nihilistic boyfriend," sighed Frida.

Frida had traded the Conservatorium for a degree in international relations. She remained a recipe for a panic attack. We were always on different wavelengths. That's the kind of thing you only see in hindsight: she was in the prime of my life, but I was never in the prime of hers.

"Just because I'm super busy doesn't mean that I'm about to break up with you, ya flake," said Frida. "I love you, remember?"

Unfortunately, love wasn't enough. The simple impulses of a summer fling in the country couldn't be reheated in the city.

I waited until we were driving back to Toowoomba on Easter Saturday to have an existential crisis.

"Can we *please* stop for hash browns?" said Frida.

"No," I said. "Maybe if you didn't get shit-faced last night, so we weren't running half an hour late ..."

"Okay, old man."

Outside Gatton, the flags of Australia and McDonald's flapped at matching altitudes. I flicked my indicator.

"Praise the Lord," said Frida. "It's an Easter miracle."

I took a piss that felt like a prayer to God, lingering a minute, pins and needles in my feet and fingers. When I returned, Frida was in the front seat, eating hash browns.

"Dude," she said. "What's the matter?"

"I don't think we're compatible," I answered.

She spat salt and saturated fat against the glass. "Is this because I was running late?"

"No. I've been thinking about it for a month."

"So you're breaking up with me?" she asked.

"Yeah. I think so. I don't want to have this chat tomorrow."

For the rest of the trip, we performed an autopsy of our second failed stab at a relationship.

"Can we stop by your house?" asked Frida.

"Yeah, I guess," I said. "Why?"

"We're not going to my place for breakup sex."

"I thought that only happened in movies."

"For a reason. It's the best."

We drove through the intersection where the mother and her son had been swept to their death at the start of January. A roadside bouquet was skewered with faded flags left over from Australia Day. The gardens at Queens Park and the War Memorial were more scenic than ever before.

"Everything is beautiful again," said Frida.

"For some."

After the flood, a widowed single father had criticised bystanders for idly watching the floodwaters drown his family. Many of the same gossipers spreading untrue rumours about him had recently attended a flood fundraiser at the showgrounds. Prince William arrived to gleeful chants of *WIL-LY! WIL-LY! WIL-LY!* It was the final stop on the "Disaster Down Under" tour.

"Look on the bright side," she said.

In my bedroom, we made out with the same intensity as during the game of spin the bottle at Nick's place.

"What are you thinking about?" asked Frida.

I was thinking about how, two years earlier, Henry was pressuring me to message Frida. That night, we walked from Mount Lofty to Queens Park to the Australian Gospel Music Festival.

I started weeping uncontrollably. Frida hugged me and said, "It'll be okay," until she realised that I was upset about griefs far deeper than a breakup. Of course being with Frida was an anticlimax: she couldn't make me seventeen again.

"I just want to go back," I said.

"Go back where?" asked Frida. "To Brisbane?"

"To before the car crash happened."

"Oh, Lech. So do I. But this is it."

Frida didn't lie everything would be fine. She embraced me patiently and waited for the tide of sorrow to subside, a private kindness inside a public tragedy.

The Soul
Is a Black Box

D OM'S TRIAL WAS SET FOR the dying weeks of winter
2011. After class, I saw a police car parked on my leafy
street in St. Lucia. I knew that they were here to deliver
the court summons, but I felt no panic, just mild relief. The
couriers were laidback. I was named as a witness, not the front-
seat passenger.

"Thanks for coming," I said.

I caught the elevator while reading the charges against
Dom: *dangerous operation of a motor vehicle causing three counts
of death and two counts of grievous bodily harm.* There'd been
a one-in-seven chance of me not being killed, disabled, or
charged with a serious crime. The car crash hadn't happened
to me, not in the same way as to the others.

"If they put that kid in the clink," said my father on the
phone, "they'll have to lock up half the country! I've done far
worse things than him."

On a nondescript Tuesday morning, I awoke from broken
sleep and sped west. The justice system had paid for petrol and
two nights off work. The blurry sun had no bite, rising behind
the bumper and making everything in the windshield seem
especially unreal.

I parked between Queens Park and the War Memorial. Photographers assembled outside the courthouse for one last hurrah. They took a few desultory pictures of me, but saved most of the film for Dom.

Inside, bereaved family members clung together. The comparatively relaxed first responders made conversation with the police and paramedics. Everyone watched the stairs for the arrival of the driver.

Dom's face was blank and freshly shaven.

"Good luck," I whispered.

Witnesses were forbidden to sit in the courtroom except while giving evidence. Nick was in the same situation, and we reunited in the waiting room. Unlike me, he couldn't remember a single thing from the night of the accident. This was a different kind of dismay: knowing too much versus missing information.

"How've you been, Lechtor?" he asked.

"Good," I said.

Nick had forgotten the drunken fights and slights behind each other's back during our final months of school. But that alone couldn't explain my inability to sit and talk openly to my oldest mate. I was capable of spilling my guts to a room of graduate students, but not to Nick. There was too much history between us. He revealed a side of me that I wanted to deny had ever existed.

"I saw that article about you getting done for drunk driving," he said.

"Yeah."

"Thanks for taking the heat off me, bro."

I had to laugh. Nick had appeared at the courthouse a few weeks before me, charged with "occasioning grievous bodily harm." In the food court of Grand Central, Nick had crossed paths with an internet troll who had mocked his injuries on Facebook a few months after the accident. The troll placed his hands on an imaginary steering wheel and mimed losing control. Nick punched him in the side of skull, busting his eardrum and drawing blood.

"I go to the pub waiting for someone to say something," said Nick. "So I can headbutt them. When I've got a brain injury."

For a glorious period in his youth, Nick was worshipped for sublime athletic performances. Now he was nostalgic for his lost popularity and prestige. This led to an aggressive streak that had never been present when he was unquestionably the best.

"I wouldn't be too hard on yourself," I said. "You've had a rough trot."

"I don't want your sympathy, dude."

The bailiff saved me from patronising him further. He mispronounced my Polish name at the courtroom door. I drifted into the witness box. It was stunning that a room united by doom could generate such a disciplined silence.

The judge offered a Bible, but I made a non-religious affirmation. The prosecution cued the footage from Henry's mobile phone. The courtroom gasped at hearing the rendition of "Wonderwall." I listened to Will's last breaths, so fast in real life and slow in my recurring dreams.

The prosecutor wanted answers. I stuck to the same script: *I remember seeing the trees. I thought we were driving into a yard. Headlights came out of nowhere.* I testified that I knew there were extra passengers before we left, indicating that the driver did, too. But I remained vague about the details. I genuinely hadn't been paying attention. *I don't remember. Maybe. I believe so. It happened very quickly.*

"No more questions, Your Honour," said the prosecutor.

"I invite cross-examination of the witness," said the judge.

Dom's defence lawyer grilled me much more vigorously than the prosecutor. The legal strategy was to plant seeds of doubt in the jury about whether Dom knew there were two passengers in the trunk. The barrister recited passages from statements I couldn't remember making.

"I can't specifically recall saying that," I said, shredding my credibility as a witness. "But I wouldn't doubt the validity of the statement."

"No more questions for Mr. Blaine," said the barrister.

"The witness is excused," said the judge.

My testimony was followed by two forensic investigators. I had to wait to read their evidence in the *Toowoomba Chronicle* the next morning. The driver had recorded a blood-alcohol reading of 0.00, they said. He was travelling at roughly 94 kilometres an hour in a 100 zone. The back tire drifted onto a gravel driveway, spinning out, a lapse that lasted approximately 0.7 to 0.8 of a second. It took less than three seconds for the accident to happen. The collision wasn't caused by a drag-racing drunk driver or a homicidal passenger grabbing the wheel. This was a catastrophic moment of inattentiveness and overcorrection.

The headline didn't read: SOBER DRIVER WAS UNDER THE SPEED LIMIT. It read: VIDEO FOOTAGE PLAYED AT TRIAL.

• • • •

THE PENDULUM SWUNG between guilt and innocence among radio listeners. On Wednesday afternoon, the jury was taken on a tour of the New England Highway. News photographers snapped pictures of the court-appointed bystanders stranded on the blacktop. A minibus ferried them back to the courthouse for closing arguments.

The defence said that the collision was a tragic accident, but the driver was innocent. The prosecution said that Dom had allowed the car to be overloaded. Someone needed to be held legally responsible. He was guilty.

On Wednesday night, I drove past Downlands to Dom's place in Mount Lofty, for the last supper before the verdict. I parked alongside the rifle range and koala sanctuary across the road from his parents' dream home. It had been remortgaged to pay for their son's legal fees. His mum fretfully prepared a roast dinner. Dom and I sat on the front patio.

"I just want it to be over," he said. "I don't care if I go away."

"What does your lawyer think?" I asked.

"Seven to eight years. But that's fine."

Seven years would see him released from prison by twenty-five. It seemed like a gap year compared to disability and death. The lucky part wasn't just climbing from the window without a scratch, but that I wasn't following him to jail: I was equally guilty of whatever moral offence Dom committed.

Before dinner, I helped Dom unspool a layer of giant bubble wrap across the swimming pool. A pool cleaner chugged through the chlorine.

"I just wish I could say that it was a stupid mistake," he said. "Without incriminating myself. But my lawyer doesn't want me to say anything."

"Why?" I asked.

"It could get twisted the wrong way, I guess."

Survivor's guilt and criminal guilt were different.

We ate greedily, pleased to be doing something meaningless with our mouths. Over dinner, Dom asked if I was seeing anyone. I lied that I was over Frida. He told me about a potential flame.

"She's keen," he said. "But let's see what happens tomorrow." The gleam in his tired eyes disappeared.

It was one thing to discuss the prospect of incarceration, but we still couldn't talk freely about what it was like to be in a collision that killed three people. Death eclipsed the animal technology of lungs and tongues and lips.

"Thanks for coming over," said Dom.

I felt an urge to touch him in some way, but resisted.

"No worries, mate," I said. "I'm here, no matter what."

"Cheers, Blaine Train. I'll be all right."

The line came out more like a whine than a roar.

When the verdict was handed down the next day, I was seventy-five miles away. A professor was discussing the development of the twenty-four-hour news cycle. My iPhone vibrated. I rushed from the room and took in the breaking news:

NOT GUILTY

Three counts of dangerous driving causing death: NOT GUILTY. Two counts of dangerous driving causing grievous bodily harm: NOT GUILTY. One count of overloading: NOT GUILTY.

The final newspaper article in the sequence on the crash finished with an optimistic plot twist:

> For much of the three days of evidence the driver sat quietly in the dock with head bowed as the most painful moments of his young life were aired in open court. And that quiet, dignified demeanour remained yesterday when the jury brought back not guilty verdicts to charges of dangerous driving causing death and grievous bodily harm... The driver left the court declining to speak to waiting media, preferring to now hopefully get on with his life.

I skipped the bus and wandered along the river in the comfortable dusk of a Brisbane winter.

Congratulations mate, I wrote to Dom with a knot in my stomach.

Why did I feel so numb, even when something good happened for once? Had I subconsciously been yearning for punishment? The life of a survivor is an anticlimax. We feel like flakes and failures and fakes, the same as everyone else, except the stakes become much higher.

I smelled butter chicken wafting down the hallway before I reached my apartment. Vincent and Anna were in the kitchen cooking dinner. On the balcony, I sat with a salivating Big Red. He applauded as the curries were served. The four of us toasted Dom's innocence, but didn't dwell on the technicalities.

"Do you feel different?" asked Vincent.

"Not particularly," I said.

It didn't matter what the jury decided, or if the public agreed with the verdict. The trial provided a legal answer to an existential question. I couldn't unsee the abyss, or unfeel the grief.

"It's still shit, isn't it?" said Big Red.

"Yeah," I said. "Unfortunately."

The skyline climbed above the slimy mangroves and hireable bicycles across the water in Orleigh Park. A CityCat ferry skidded on the black water. Fruit bats flapped in the opposite direction, flying back towards the university.

Human beings chase yardsticks in the distance, until passing those markers and seeing that the dark feelings we were fleeing from are actually part of us. The trick was to stop striving so damn hard to be alive. To laugh and fuck and love *till death do us part* from a bargain that I never asked to receive. And to fight the urge for flight, even when my body told me it was time to leave.

• • • •

I SAW NICK ONCE in the next seven years, at a twenty-first birthday party. He had a job painting trucks, and was friends with a cast of rugby-league-playing public-school boys who didn't judge his rough edges.

On May 2, 2018—the ninth anniversary of the car crash—I sent him a Facebook message. I was back living in Toowoomba for the first time since school. *Hey mate, thinking of you today. How's life been? We should catch up.*

We arranged to meet for lunch on a Saturday afternoon. Nick didn't have a licence, so I punched his address into Google Maps. He lived one hundred yards from my new share house.

"You have arrived at the destination," said the GPS unit almost immediately.

A pool in the front yard was filled with leaves. Nick answered the door with paint in his crooked eyebrows, voice lower and slower than I remembered. Now a father of two, he had put on some weight since the court case. The silent house behind him looked to be filled with toys and fast-food wrappers.

"Nick," I said.

"Hey, Lechtor," he said. "You look good, man. How are ya?"

I had grey hair and the unintentional suntan of a marathon runner. I jogged thirty miles a week as a pre-emptive strike against my father's diabetes and my mother's melancholy.

"I live around the corner from here," I said.

We shook hands for the second time in quick succession, chuckling at the odds, two grown men who knew everything and nothing about each other.

"Well, bloody hell," he said. "It's a small world, isn't it?"

"Small world!"

I drove us to a café across the road from Grammar in my brand-new Mitsubishi Outlander. Schoolboy rugby union was underway across the road. I ordered a chicken Caesar wrap and strong flat white. Nick got the same.

"I need to lose some weight," he said. "What's your secret?"

"I started running marathons," I said. "It clears my head."

"From what?"

I told Nick that I was writing a book about the accident.

"Why?" he asked. Not angry or defensive, just intrigued.

The truth was that I'd been born a writer, and this was the most important story I could tell at the present moment. I told Nick that I also wanted to raise awareness of depression.

"You're *still* depressed?" he asked, gobsmacked, mentally comparing that disclosure with Facebook images of me grinning at black-tie balls in Brisbane.

"Well, yeah," I said. "I still see a psychologist once a month."

Nick kept looking over his shoulder at the upper-class mums. I paid for lunch and suggested a stroll around Queens Park.

The peonies loosened Nick up. He filled in the gaps since high school. He got hooked on pot and video games, blowing out to 240 pounds, so anxious and ashamed that he didn't make it outside for his twenty-first birthday. The quickest fix for the endless cycle of lethargy and self-loathing was crystal meth.

"Ice stopped me from dreaming about death," he said.

We walked back to the four-wheel drive, and talked more as I drove up to Picnic Point. Nick kept trying to quit meth cold turkey. But the problem with getting in so deep was that he didn't have any friends left who weren't addicts or dealers. Relapse was accompanied by the adrenaline rush of belonging.

"It's scary," he said. "These people were scared of *me*."

We drove around for over an hour. I lifted the handbrake outside Nick's house. He asked for my advice.

"Mate, I'm pretty sure you've got depression," I said.

"Do you think so?"

"If it walks like a duck. And quacks like a duck."

"But I don't want to go on those drugs, man."

In some ways, I was lucky I'd flamed out so young and publicly. A judge forced me to get the help that I might've otherwise sidestepped. My sister's psychology degree destigmatised a process that had once seemed weak.

"I've been on a medication called Pristiq for eight years," I said. "And now I'm on another antidepressant called Valdoxan that helps me sleep. They don't fix all of my problems. But they give me the ability to address them."

Nick nodded. There was less tension in our goodbye handshake than in the first two. I moved back to Brisbane, and didn't see him in person for another eighteen months. But he started on Citalopram a few days later. I'd given him permission.

thanks mate, he messaged me. *best thing I've ever done.*

• • • •

TWO WEEKS BEFORE the tenth anniversary, I was cruising on the Warrego Highway, heading to be the best man at Vincent and Anna's wedding. The ceremony was to be at Downlands, where I had given a eulogy for Henry a decade ago.

The Commonwealth Bank—where my father used to launder gambling profits through my account—had been renovated into a strip club called The Vault. The Metropole Hotel was about to be demolished. The Country Club Hotel had burnt down in suspicious circumstances after the owner, a former rugby league player, was arrested for cocaine trafficking.

That nuptial morning, I idled beside the house that my father and I had renovated. A sign announced it was due to be replaced by luxury villas.

Around the corner, Vincent pushed a green-lidded wheelie bin filled with offcuts from the floral archway. He'd barely added a wrinkle since high school, and had the same quizzical grin.

"Hey, Blainey," he said.

"Hey, Vin Diesel," I said. "It's great to be here."

I had completely missed the planned rehearsal.

"You know why they call you Blisters?" asked Vincent.

"No. Why?"

"Because you turn up after all the work is done."

Vincent had no idea that I was dying inside. Today was just a wedding. Downlands was just a high school. The looming anniversary didn't trigger physical trepidation for him. He knew pretty much everything about me, but the strangeness of my return hadn't occurred to him. I wasn't just a survivor.

We walked inside. Tiny footsteps thudded down the hallway. A blonde two-year-old named Billie jumped into my arms without asking for permission. I was her atheist godfather. She had Vincent's dimple in her chin. I always felt calm when I was with Billie, even when she pinched my skin or punched me in the nuts. She didn't compare me with a lost version of myself.

"Lech!" she said, a mouthful of teeth now.

I spent the next half-hour trying to help Billie locate items that she apparently needed with some urgency: MY HAT! MY BALL! MY BOOK! When we found the coveted object, she lost any desire to have it.

"Mummy, Daddy, and Lech!" Billie sang with a secret logic.

"Lech's not getting married to us, honey," said Anna.

Anna kissed me briskly on the cheek. She whisked a screaming Billie away to get ready with the bridal party. Vincent handed me the rings. The rest of the groom's party arrived. We showered and fumbled with each other's bowties. Spotify played "Streets of Your Town" by the Go-Betweens.

Outside, it was a dark afternoon. Everyone fretted about the prospect of a wet wedding. The groomsmen filed into an Uber. Vincent rode shotgun with me. Drizzle fell on the Mort Estate, and we glided towards a fog-swamped Mount Lofty. Not everything had changed: Downlands still looked like Hogwarts; I still felt like an imposter.

"Are you all right, Blainey?" asked Vincent.

"I'm hanging in there," I said.

The grieving process is eternally incomplete. My defences were still undone by the smallest triggers: the smell of Lynx deodorant, the taste of cheap beers, the opening chords of "Wonderwall," breaking news about traffic accidents, doppelgängers at shopping centres.

I noticed the gaps at eighteenth and twenty-first birthdays. Now, at baptisms and weddings, I glimpsed the grinning faces of children who'd never understand the wistfulness crippling their guardians when reminded of Will, Hamish, and Henry, who'd eventually be gone for longer than they were alive.

Vincent and I walked the naked acre to join everyone else. The crowd migrated from the dining room to the lawn. Elders claimed seating at the front. The young and unmarried hovered at the back. We were the best and worst parts of our mothers and fathers, a mixture of dimples and addictions. The dresses and suits were more expensive, but the emotional landscape was basically the same as at a high-school formal.

Rain pitter-pattered on the umbrella that I lifted above Vincent.

"Put it away," he said. "It's not even raining that hard."

The bride arrived in a convoy of Range Rovers. The hipster celebrant cued "Into My Arms" by Nick Cave & the Bad Seeds on Spotify. Billie jumped from the back seat. She squeezed a white rose.

An unassuming bride and groom were pronounced husband and wife. The sky was silver and slightly orange in the west. I scribbled my signature as a witness.

I carried Billie from the lawn to the courtyard for refreshments. The tails of her white dress were streaked with mud. We walked along the driveway beside the Garden of Remembrance. I listened to the trickle of water from Henry's fountain.

"Lech!" said Billie. The sound of her voice pronouncing my name without tripping over the silent *h* was a gift from Vincent. My guilt was eclipsed by gratitude.

The reception was in the same building as Henry's wake. After dinner, the MC called me to the podium. I told a simple story about human evolution: two oversensitive youngest children, who became best friends after a car crash.

"Vincent made me braver by being an individual," I said. "And he gave me permission to grieve by setting an example of vulnerability."

The audience laughed and cried. Nobody seemed freaked out by the admissions of imperfection. We all run from ghosts that no one else can see.

After the slow dance, the audience stormed the floor. Men waltzed with men, women with women. Discs slipped attempting limbo. Wine splattered across the linoleum. Mops were fetched from the kitchen.

"I love you, mate," said Vincent during a quiet moment.

"I love you too," I said.

The reception ended at midnight. Floodlights illuminated the gloom outside. We waited for Ubers on the New England Highway. Fog blew from the dining room to the roadside shrine.

How does someone keep confronting this abyss without succumbing to nihilism? I built a tapestry of attachments to people whose voices were louder than the pessimistic head noises whispering that no one would miss me.

• • • •

FOR THE TENTH ANNIVERSARY of the crash, I organised dinner with Tim. That afternoon, under glum skies, I went for a run around the Brisbane River. The Story Bridge was lit green. Peak-hour traffic rumbled above me. I sprinted smugly past the suits drinking knock-off cocktails on Eagle Street Pier.

At 7:00 PM, I became one of them. Frida and Big Red waited at a table. Frida wore a short black dress with red lipstick, her brown hair in a bob.

"You have short hair," I said.

"You have grey hair," she said.

"Touché."

"At least you have hair," said Big Red.

His head was clean-shaven. Big Red had retired from contact sport due to concussion. He worked on a gas mine out west. Frida was a left-wing staffer for the Labor Party, taking the career path that I'd mapped out in school. And she was better at it, more attracted to policy work than ego fulfilment.

"I always thought you were the political one," Big Red said to me.

"So did I," I said.

"His skin was too thin for politics," said Frida, who was dating a thick-skinned solicitor. I got along with all of her boyfriends like a house on fire.

My mixed emotions were halted by Tim's arrival. Laughter followed him from the entrance to the dinner table, intensifying when he spied Big Red across the room. Tim still couldn't walk or talk, but he had the same bright blue eyes, wide smile, and mouthful of straight teeth. A male disability worker pushed the wheelchair to the table before decamping to get his client a Corona and lime. Tim was here for a good time.

"You look so handsome, Tim," said Frida, kissing him on the cheek.

Tim locked my palm in a handshake that would have made my father blush. He pulled me into a bear hug that I couldn't break free from, proving once and for all who remained the alpha male.

"Ring the bell!" I shouted. "I submit!"

Big Red gave his first child—a ginger-haired behemoth like him—the middle name "Timothy" as a tribute to one of his best mates. Now Tim tried to physically overpower the biggest person in the room as he had me.

"I'm sick of your shit, Timmy," said Big Red, rolling his sleeves up. "I'm here for a civilised evening. But I am willing to put you in a sleeper hold."

This brought a fresh round of howls. We ordered pizzas. Tim signalled for another round while listening intently. He frowned when the subject matter grew more serious, and cracked up at punchlines. Tim had six nieces and nephews. I had twelve of them. We were both the funny uncle: he was funny ha-ha, and I was a bit funny sometimes. Would I have been so forgiving if it were me in the wheelchair and him living freely?

But Tim didn't want pity. He went to Brisbane Broncos games on Friday nights and Pentecostal church on Sundays. He owned a home in the suburbs with a pool and had travelled to twenty countries. All he needed was me to spin him a yarn.

I retold the story—how many times now?—of the night a drunken Big Red was led from my granny flat to the house by Tim, who noticed that my mother was in the toilet. So he promptly directed Big Red into her empty bedroom.

"It was an absolute stitch-up," said Big Red.

I sat at the dinner table with my oldest friends, winded by the blissful follies of youth, while ignoring the holy disappointments of adulthood.

"This has been the best night in forever," said Frida.

Tim yawned through the laughter. His carer called it a night. We did a farewell round of handshakes and hugs. Bolder stories were told. It came up that Frida had recently broken up with the solicitor. This was news to me. Her knee knocked on mine like a locked door. Pretty soon, it was just the two of us and Big Red at the table, as the bar passed closing time.

"Catch ya later, legends," said Big Red.

Frida and I caught an Uber across the Go Between Bridge to her art deco apartment in West End. In the living room, there was a painting on an easel of a topless woman sucking a lollipop. "It's me," said Frida. "*Self-Portrait at Twenty-Seven.*"

Throughout our twenties, Frida and I occasionally became single at the same time. We would hook up and idly contemplate giving it another crack, until one of us met someone else, where the stakes weren't quite so high.

"I'm glad I became a writer," I said, continuing my inner monologue from dinner. Frida didn't need me to provide further context.

"You were always a weirdo," Frida said. "Chasing ya dad's dream. And taking for granted all of the things that actually make you so great."

I got myself a beer. Frida changed into pyjama shorts and poured a glass of wine. We kissed without impatience. Neither of us was going anywhere. She let me borrow her electric toothbrush, replacing the taste of pizza with Colgate.

Afterwards, we lay next to each other, pleasantly empty.

"I wish I enjoyed sex that much when we were together," I said.

"That's what everyone thinks when they're single. Sleep on it."

But I was no longer gripped by the deep conviction that I'd recapture the past by being with Frida. This was it.

• • • •

AROUND THE CORNER from Downlands College, I sat with Nick and Dom at the start of January 2020. It was the halfway mark of Australia's Black Summer bushfires. The three of us hadn't been alone together since we were seventeen. Nick had been clean for eighty-six days, the longest dry spell of his wet twenties.

"It's a mantra: *om mani padme hum,*" he said, explaining the seven chakras of Hinduism, and the new tattoo of a Kundalini serpent twisting along his ripped, tanned forearm. "I repeat it to myself every morning."

Nick had got out of rehab the day before. He was bright-eyed and forty-five pounds lighter than when we had met at Queens Park. The former high-school football star had gained a sense of Zen from a program of weightlifting and group therapy.

"Rehab's just a bunch of blokes talking about their demons," he said.

Dom was a born-again communist with a blond ponytail and twin nose piercings. He showed Nick the tattoo on his skinny wrist of a Dreamtime rain spirit, passed onto him by an Aboriginal mate named Sam.

"I stopped ignoring what happened," said Dom, who rarely drank anymore. "And I accepted it."

The unpatriotic American wore a hammer and sickle T-shirt given to him by a Vietnamese violinist at an ashram in southern India. For two years, he had consumed magic mushrooms and learned the language of self-compassion.

"Well, I feel like a real conformist," I said. "I've never meditated or done psychedelics. And I don't have a single tattoo."

"I'll give you a tattoo," said Dom, who had ten of them.

"I promised my dad that I'd be a cleanskin," I said.

"Pussy," said Nick.

I watched Dom etch Nick's middle finger with the tattoo of an arrow. The Department of Defence was about to start subdividing the rifle range and koala sanctuary into 342 quarter-acre blocks, and the roadside shrine was about to get displaced by a cycle path.

"You need to carve out some inner peace," Nick said to me.

"That's why I went to India and Iran," said Dom. "Australians are so uncomfortable talking about pain. Other cultures confront it. We just go to the pub and get smashed together. How is that the definition of toughness?"

Nick shadowboxed to prove that he'd got the knack back. He confessed to suffering a recurring nightmare about getting bathed in the hospital by strangers.

"I feel like I woke up from the coma yesterday," he said. "Nurses wiping my arse for me. It was so embarrassing. But I couldn't tell anyone that."

Dom, a vegan, cooked tofu and pineapple on a barbeque. He flipped them onto focaccias with avocado, spinach, and kimchi. At the tipping point of the Great Dividing Range, we sat on the front patio, chewing the fat about depression and post-traumatic stress disorder without breaking eye contact.

"I finally forgave myself," said Dom.

Nick offered us cigarettes. I stopped smoking when I became a runner, but I lit one up for old time's sake. My lungs didn't digest the relapse with dignity. I coughed harder than the first night Nick and I did shots of Dad's Scotch and fleeced some menthol cigarettes from my snoring mum's bedside drawer, thirteen-year-olds determined to become grown men overnight.

"I've missed you guys," he said.

Nick took a call from the mother of his children, a subtle reminder that he had much more on his plate than either of us. He hugged Dom and me without any trace of discomfort.

"Does writing about it help?" asked Nick.

"Not exactly," I said. "I'll be psyched to finish the book."

"Why?" asked Dom. "So you can wake people up?"

"No," I said. "So I can go back to sleep."

"I don't think it's going anywhere, bro," said Nick.

There was no closure. Trauma doesn't allow for a heart-warming moment of redemption. We kept persisting anyway, epic vessels of emotion, less of a danger to ourselves and more of an open secret to those around us.

Acknowledgments

*C*AR CRASH: A MEMOIR OF THE AFTERMATH is a work of creative nonfiction, not journalism, reportage, or a personal diary. Scenes have been re-created based on my memories, which are fallible—and were even before I suffered from a major trauma. At times, secondary events and characters have been streamlined to avoid confusing the reader with too much information. Vincent and Frida are composites of real people. This was done not just to simplify the narrative, but also to maintain the real individuals' privacy.

It simply isn't feasible to acknowledge everyone who has helped me personally since the accident, or professionally since I started to write about it. *Car Crash* is a tribute to those who've supported my writing career. My survival is the best possible testament to the people who've provided me with friendship.

As editor, nobody's eyes have been more focused on my sentences and paragraphs than the vociferously supportive Julia Carlomagno, whose patience and empathy under pressure have been saintly. As publisher at Black Inc., Chris Feik's quiet confidence in my prose has been the greatest game-changer of my professional development. My thanks go as well to the team at Greystone Books for creating this international edition.

Nick Feik—editor of *The Monthly*—turned this one-trick memoirist into a journalist. He has made me a much better writer. I owe Morry Schwartz a huge debt for creating the publications that have given me so much intellectual sustenance, first as a teenage reader, and now—somehow—as a member of the Schwartz Media stable.

At the University of Queensland, Chris Somerville and Jack Vening told me to take writing seriously. Ash Hanson from *Kill Your Darlings* was my first source of editorial feedback for the earliest draft of *Car Crash*. Scribe Publications shortlisted an excerpt of that draft for their Scribe Nonfiction Prize for Young Writers in 2016—the awards ceremony was where I first met Julia. Aviva Tuffield sent an email out of the blue asking me to send her the excerpt.

Julianne Schultz, John Tague, and Ash Hay from *Griffith Review* have been endlessly encouraging, and provided a regular home for my prose. In 2017, I received funding from a Queensland Literary Award, and undertook a mentorship with Kristina Olsson, whose infatuation with language was contagious.

Agent Benython Oldfield recruited me to Zeitgeist Media. He's been a boundless sounding board since.

In 2017, I was lucky enough to meet Bri Lee, who inspired me to keep going, while making me feel as though I belonged to a kindred community of writers. Laura Elvery offered friendship and deft editing suggestions. Benjamin Law has become one of my most effusive champions. Helen Garner generously made time to read, and offered ruthless but illuminating critical feedback.

Thank you to Jessica Sullivan for designing such a beautiful cover. Thank you to Archie Hamilton for cheering me on thirty seconds before the full-time hooter.

Greg Manthey and Andrew Fellenberg, human beings first and high-school teachers second, helped guide me through the aftermath of the car accident. Stephen Shaw saw a spark of creativity amid the darkness. He insisted that I pull my finger out. Thank you to Robert for your charitable contribution to my mental wellbeing.

The St. Mary's and Downlands seniors of 2009 hold a special place in my heart. Alice provided so much thankless sensitivity. Matt and Hayden read the earliest drafts of *Car Crash* and showed their souls to me, so that my confidence in the need for this project could grow. Georgia offered critical feedback and hours of reminiscence. Macca and Kev deserve a special mention for their unwavering mateship.

Thank you to Tim, Nick, and Dom for letting me tell your stories. Thank you to Melissa for your consistent wisdom. Thank you to Linda for your shining kindness. Thank you to Nicole, Courtney, Erin, Sam, and Tess for revisiting a difficult period.

Tom and Lenore Blaine won't be alive to read *Car Crash*, but it wouldn't exist without his gift of self-belief or her gift of literature. I'm forever indebted to their decision to foster Steven, John, Rebecca, and Hannah, whose own families have helped me endure the grief of our parents' passing. The six of them are my biggest influences. Hannah has been my loudest cheerleader and staunchest source of love.